THE OFFICIAL
SUNDAY SCHOOL TEACHERS HANDBOOK

How to Succeed in Sunday School By Trying Just a Little Bit Harder

by
JOANNE OWENS

Illustrated by
LAFE LOCKE

MERIWETHER PUBLISHING LTD.
COLORADO SPRINGS, COLORADO

Meriwether Publishing Ltd., Publisher
P.O. Box 7710
Colorado Springs, CO 80933

Cover Design & Cartoon Illustrations: Lafe Locke
Inside Design: Michelle Zapel Gallardo
Typesetter: Sharon Garlock
Executive Editor: Arthur Zapel

ISBN: 0916260-42-9
© Copyright MCMLXXXVII Meriwether Publishing Ltd.
Printed in the United States of America
First Edition
Third Printing
Library of Congress #87-043102

To the Covenant Class, the world's finest Sunday school class, to my favorite class member, my husband, L.P. and to my friend and fellow writer, Ginny Reese.

ACKNOWLEDGEMENTS

Thanks or apologies

. . . *to all those Sunday school teachers whose classes I have enjoyed or endured down through the years. Believe me, I learned more from you than you'll ever know.*

. . . *to my friends, John Brown, Sue Clark, Marion Collins, Victor Floyd, Beth, Andrew, Mary Catherine, Patrick and William Goble, Drenna Hollingsworth, Bert Lance, Lindi Lewis, Lee Linn, Janet Litherland, Becky, William, Helen and Susan Mathews, David Peek, Sara and J. D. Pollard, Carlton Pridgen, Mike Scott and Mary Smith, for providing encouragement, photographs or information.*

. . . *to the following individuals and organizations for their assistance:*

The H. J. Heinze Company

The Rockefeller Archive Center

The National Archives

Senator John Glenn

Minnie Pearl

*Graded Press Board of Discipleship,
    United Methodist Church.*

INTRODUCTION

Sunday school was a part of my life since my early childhood. As a girl in Centerville, Tennessee, I listened to many a Sunday school lesson and came under the influence of a variety of teachers. (I wish some of them had had Joanne Owens' book to help them perk up their classes!)

During my young adult years, I too was a Sunday school teacher, so I can identify with all of you who are now teaching a class. You deserve lots of stars in your crown. Teaching Sunday school is a tough but rewarding task. It can also be lots of fun, and it definitely can be the source of many laughs.

Joanne Owens has not only found the humor in Sunday school, but she has written a book crammed full of ideas and suggestions to help you be a better Sunday school teacher. This book will entertain, inform, and tickle you as it helps you become a better Sunday school teacher.

God bless you all. Keep up the good work in Sunday school.

Minnie Pearl
Star of the Grand Old Opry
Nashville, Tennessee

Just about everybody loves it!

66 *Never have I read anyone with a keener insight into the needs and interests of children.* **99**

Mother Goose

66 *Ah, my soul rejoices in the gems of wisdom found in <u>The Official Sunday School Teachers Handbook</u>.* **99**

King Solomon

66 *A masterpiece! I completely lost my head over <u>The Official Sunday School Teachers Handbook</u>.* **99**

Anne Boleyn

66 *I think I'm in love with Joanne Owens.* **99**

Prince Charming

66 *There's no doubt about it, <u>The Official Sunday School Teachers Handbook</u> could have solved all my problems.* **99**

Job

PREFACE

If you're reading this book, you can probably thank a Sunday school teacher. It is written in tribute to all those faithful men and women who could have slept late on Sunday mornings, but who chose the more arduous path.

Those of us who have grown up in the Sunday school regard it as family, so we feel comfortable and secure enough to laugh at its lighter side. When we do, we are laughing at ourselves. What could be healthier?

It is the hope and prayer of the author that those who read this book will celebrate the Sunday school, help to make it better, and have fun while doing it.

TABLE OF CONTENTS

Chapter 1:
VOLUNTEER
OF THE YEAR

Sunday school teachers have inspired, challenged, and bored us all. We have loved them, had our lives changed by them, and sometimes avoided them. Sunday school teachers have made us feel special, worthwhile, accepted and guilty as a yard dog on the sofa. Their tireless teaching has kept us in church and out of reform school. They frowned at us when we passed Life Savers and notes down the pew, and they hugged us when we became full members of the church. With no pay and precious little gratitude from anyone, these unsung, dedicated workers have taught, loved and prayed for us. Most of us owe whatever spirituality and religious knowledge we possess to Sunday school teachers. Many of us can honestly say, "I am what I am because of Sunday school."

If there had been such a thing as *Volunteer of the Year in* 1780 in Gloucester, England, the award would surely have gone to printer and publisher Robert Raikes. He started Sunday school classes for poor, neglected children, who without protection of child labor laws worked six days a week in the town's pin factory. Raikes gathered ruffians from the city streets and turned their cursing, fighting and thievery into Bible-reading, prayers and hymnsinging. Today we Sunday school teachers agonize over a 45-minute lesson. Raikes' classes lasted from 10 a.m. until 5 p.m., with an hour off at noon.

With no public education in England at the time, the masses were illiterate. Raikes taught children to read and write so they could read the Bible for themselves. He rented Mrs. Meredith's kitchen to hold classes. Alas, the students behaved so terribly that poor Mrs. Meredith couldn't take it, so Raikes moved his school to the home of Mrs. Critchley, who taught the girls in one room while Raikes taught the boys in another. He used every trick he could think of to motivate and discipline. Good behavior was rewarded with Bibles, books, games, clothing and shoes. In time, Raikes' classes evolved from "ragged schools" to Bible schools for children, to religious instruction for people of all ages.

There are others who deserve credit for starting Sunday schools. In Scotland, as far back as 1560, the clergy, and later volunteers, held classes on the Sabbath for catechising the young and ignorant. In 1763, Hannah Ball, a pious Methodist lady, gathered a "wild little company" in her home for Sunday instruction. While a missionary in Georgia, John Wesley taught children in Sunday classes as early as 1735.

The Sunday school grew by leaps and bounds in the 19th century. The typical old-fashioned Sunday school was held in the auditorium where noisy opening exercises included hymnsinging, the superintendent's prayer, and the reading of the day's lesson (usually from the Uniform Series). Babies fretted, and restless children wiggled. After the assembly, the group was divided according to ages to meet in cubicles or behind curtains. After a 30-minute lesson, the bell rang, and Sunday school was dismissed.

---

*Throughout this book, the words *he, him* and *his* are intended to mean also *she, her* and *hers,* to include all people, regardless of sex.

With the twentieth century came professional Christian educators and graded lessons that took account of motivations, stages of maturity and learning ability. (That's jargon for *A little kid can understand "love one another," but he's not too swift in comprehending the complexities of the book of Revelation.)* Developmental needs of each group were stressed. For instance, we learned that young children need to smear finger paints and feel modeling clay ooze between their fingers before they are ready to sit down and fill in the blanks in a workbook. As a result of these educational developments, classrooms were built to accommodate the needs of children as well as adults. Supply catalogs were filled with teaching equipment suitable for each age, and denominational publishing houses provided tons of curriculum resources.

Also with the professional educator came the term, *church school.* For years church leaders encouraged the use of that name rather than *Sunday school* in order to stress that the value of the educational experience is not dependent on the day of the week. They said that meaningful Christian education takes place on the other six days as well as on Sunday mornings. Some of us never learned to say *church school,* and those who did are now being told to say *Sunday school* again. This is to emphasize the uniqueness of Sunday as once again a special day.

Just as the past century brought changes in educational philosophies, teaching methods, curriculum materials, and physical facilities in the Sunday school, it also brought changes in our society and lifestyles that threatened the very existence of the Sunday school. Some critics have been so pessimistic about the Sunday school as to write its obituary. But instead of dying, the Sunday school has become a vital part of our culture and the primary training ground for Christianity. Today approximately 43,000,000 children and adults attend more than 440,000 Protestant Sunday schools. Roman Catholics, Jews, and other religious groups have similar schools. The Sunday school has reached people of almost all classes, races, and denominational affiliations, and it is one of the church's greatest forces for education and evangelism. Statistics tell us that as the Sunday school goes, so goes the church.

If a feasibility study had been done on this institution before it began, the shaky plan would have been flatly turned down by any reasonable businessman. After all, the Sunday school has never received the benefit of Madison Avenue advertising or government funding. Its standards have frequently

3

been uncertain and ill-defined, and it has usually been led by untrained, unpaid personnel. The lay person has always been at the center of religious education in the church, because from the beginning, Sunday school has been a volunteer movement based on idealism and compassion, and fueled by religious zeal. Behind it all there was always the faithful, dedicated, capable Sunday school teacher. Wait a minute. Faithful? Yes. Dedicated? Yes. Capable? Well. . . sometimes.

Probably no one ever set out to be a bad Sunday school teacher, just as no one ever set out to be a bad parent. But experience and common sense indicate that there are plenty of inept people in both positions. It's easy to understand why the world has so many parents unfit for their roles. But why does the church put up with poor Sunday school teachers? Perhaps the reason is that the only thing more difficult than demanding quality work from volunteers is conferring pink slips on them.

The real miracle is that the Sunday school movement, dependent from the beginning on untrained, often poorly qualified leadership, has sustained itself for over two centuries.

Some would say commitment is the key, and that committed Christians make good Sunday school teachers. Maybe so. No one would deny the importance of Christian commitment, but if that alone were sufficient, why are there so many of our former teachers and classes that we'd just as soon forget? In the following pages, you'll meet some typical Sunday school teachers and see some of the pitfalls and unique opportunities of teaching a Sunday school class. Keep on reading, and you'll probably find yourself. You'll also learn how a typical Sunday school teacher can become a better one by trying just a little bit harder.

COULD BE YOU?

Profile of the Perfect Sunday School Teacher:

1. Has a natural talent for teaching and a loving, winning way with people.
2. Has a Master's Degree in communications skills and a Ph.D. in Christian Education.
3. Is fluent in both Hebrew and Greek, with an encyclopedic knowledge of the Bible and Middle Eastern geography.
4. Is independently wealthy. Has no need for a job and can therefore spend unlimited time on Sunday school lesson preparation and weekly visits in the homes of all class members.
5. Is attractive, enthusiastic, and above all, young.
6. Is totally mature with at least thirty years experience as a Sunday school teacher.
7. Is a single orphan — no family members to request weekend trips, get sick on Sunday, or dawdle and cause tardiness at Sunday school.
8. Has a keen insight into the problems facing contemporary families and a comprehensive understanding of the characteristics and needs of children and youth.
9. Is a marriage counselor.
10. Has sincere dedication and commitment because of being a born-again spirit-filled Christian who walks daily with the Lord in a deep and abiding personal relationship.

GUESS WHO.

Profile of the Typical Sunday School Teacher:

1. Has some personality problems of his/her own, but is working on them.
2. Has a mediocre education and thinks studying is for people who go to school.
3. *Thinks* Isaiah came after Abraham but would have to ask the preacher to be sure.
4. Works at a stressful job five days a week and does the yard and housework all day Saturday.
5. Has moderate to little teaching experience.
6. Has countless demands by parents, children spouse, and other family member who expect his/her undivided attention and support.
7. Deals with most of the problems facing families in contemporary society.
8. Often feels pain, frustration and insecurity.
9. Sometimes cries and swears. Frequently prays.
10. Loves the Lord and the church and wants to be faithful, but finds it is an uphill struggle.

Robert Raikes' Principles of Christian Education:

*(Good old Robert figured all this out without the benefit of a single course in child psychology. And he never took **Principles of Christian Education, 101-102.**)*

1. Vice in the child is an imitation of familiar sights and sounds.
2. There is a time in the child's life when it is innocent. Then the faculties are active and receptive.
3. Good seeds cannot be planted too early.
4. The child takes pleasure in being good when goodness is made attractive.

Ten Ways to Tell if You're Not Succeeding as a Sunday School Teacher:

1. No one shows up for your class.
2. Your class members vote to meet next Sunday in the mall's video game room.
3. The chairs in your Sunday school classroom turn up in the church's yard sale.
4. No one shows up for your class.
5. The preacher gives you a one-way ticket to Libya.
6. No one shows up for your class.
7. Your church's Christian Education Committee padlocks the door to your Sunday school classroom.
8. Your voice can't be heard over the snores.
9. The local judge issues a temporary restraining order against your lessons.
10. No one shows up for your class.

How to Spot a Sunday School Teacher:

A teacher of adults . . .

Can be seen studying the quarterly under the dryer at the hair dressers or while waiting at the barber shop.

Has a lean and hungry look (no time to cook on Sunday).

Wears a good suit that is liberally coated in chalk dust.

A teacher of youth. . .

Has small bits of hay (from the last hayride) clinging to his sweater.

Can be seen waiting his turn at the psychiatrist's office.

A teacher of children . . .

Drives a car filled with empty egg cartons and coffee cans (for craft time).

Has fingers beginning to grow together from continual use of hand puppets.

Has unusually limber legs from sitting in child-size chairs.

A teacher of pre-schoolers. . .

Has animal cracker crumbs in pockets.

Has fingernails permanently stained from modeling clay and fingerpaints.

Has best clothes spattered with school glue.

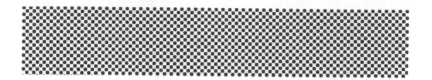

The Perfect Sunday School Class Member:

1. Attends every Sunday unless deathly ill or on honeymoon.
2. Always studies lesson.
3. Brings Bible and lesson book to class.
4. Volunteers to send cards, collect money, host the class party, mark the roll book and wash the chalkboard whenever needed.
5. Brings in supplementary helps concerning the leson, such as explanations from commentaries, pertient newspaper clippings and coffee and doughnuts for the entire class.
6. Owns a van, which he happily provides (including gas) for class field trips.
7. Is full of wisdom, patience, charm, wit, friendliness, intelligence and deep spirituality.
8. Can be called on to lead in prayer without advance notice.
9. Remembers the teacher's birthday with flowers, candy or cash.
10. Always carries extra chalk in pocket.

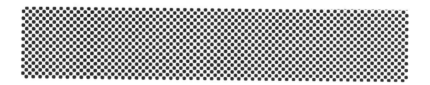

Famous Sunday School Teachers:

JOHN D. ROCKEFELLER
*Sunday School Superintendent,
Cleveland, Ohio, Teacher Men's
Bible Class, New York City*

MRS. J. D. ROCKEFELLER
*Head of the Primary Department,
Fifth Avenue Baptist Church
New York City*

H. J. HEINZE
*(Of Pickle and
Ketchup Fame)*

JOHN WANAMAKER
*Department Store Tycoon and
Postmaster General of U.S.*

CHARLES EVANS HUGHES
*Chief Justice, U.S.
Supreme Court*

JIMMY CARTER
*President of U.S.,
Teacher, Plains, Georgia
Baptist Church*

11

SOME FAMOUS PEOPLE WHO NEVER TAUGHT SUNDAY SCHOOL ✳

Front Row: **Mata Hari** *(Dancer/Spy during World War I)*. Second Row (L to R): **Genghis Khan** *(Ruthless conqueror of Mongol empire)*, **Tokyo Rose** *(Propaganda broadcaster for Japanese during World War II)*, **Fidel Castro** *(Liberator turned dictator of Cuba)*. Back Row (L to R): **Bonnie Parker** *(of bank robbery fame)*, **Adolph Hitler** *(Nazi dictator of Germany)*, **Jesse James** *(of train robbery fame)*.

*All information is either carefully researched and documented or is a product of the author's creative genius.

12

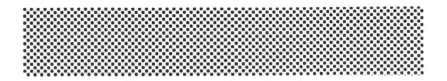

Great Sunday School Controversies:

1. Shall we separate the sexes or have co-educational classes?
2. Shall we give perfect attendance pins?
3. Shall we have assembly?
4. Shall we divide adult classes according to age?
5. Shall we use non-denominational literature?
6. Shall we encourage children to memorize scripture?
7. Shall we use Bible-centered or person-centered curriculum materials?
8. Shall we have an attendance campaign?
9. Shall we allow classes to keep their offering and spend it as they please?
10. Shall we have a Coke machine?

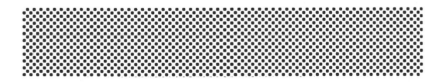

Chapter 2:
WHO SAID YOU GRADUATED?

Sunday School is for Adults,Too.

You know Miss Lillie. She's the dear sainted lady who has taught the Young Matrons' Class for almost a century. (They called the class *Young Matrons* when that name fit the status of the members. Now 75 percent of them are great-grandmothers.)

Miss Lillie took the class *temporarily* in 1902, when its regular teacher went off to be a nurse in the Spanish-American War. Unfortunately, the nurse contracted malaria and never returned, and Miss Lillie has been teaching the class ever since.

It's been rumored that Miss Lillie is 115, but no one will

ever know. She is sweet, faithful and well-meaning, with the liveliness and predictability of an aging house cat.

Miss Lillie has always used the Uniform Lesson Series, firmly believing that if it was good enough for mama, it's good enough for me.

Naturally, Miss Lillie uses the Triple L Teaching Method: Lecture, Listen and Leave. After all, the class always sits there in silence, so they must not have any ideas worth discussing. The veteran teacher's motto is *We've Always Done it This Way*. She hangs a *Do Not Disturb* sign on the classroom doorknob, and at times, there seems to be a matching sign hanging around her neck.

However, many members of the Young Matrons Class get a degree of security from the predictability of their Sunday morning ritual with Miss Lillie. They've come to depend on her lectures, and it's a good time to sit quietly and contemplate whether to have potatoes or rice with the roast beef.

PARTICIPATE OR PERISH

If a class is bland, dull and unstimulating, it's probably a sign that class members feel no responsibility for their own learning. How many times have you heard, "The teacher learns more than anyone else in the class"? People learn better when they work at it. When they think, verbalize, question and actively participate in a purposeful way, they stimulate one another, and are bound to learn more than when they sit and speculate. This is true for adults as well as children and young people.

If you want to insure a group's slow death, simply see to it that they only have to sit and listen to a speaker without getting involved. *But my class won't get involved and do anything different. They want to be spoon fed,* you might be thinking. Don't be so sure. Low participation does not necessarily mean low interest on the part of the class. But it might indicate poor leadership.

How does a Sunday school teacher deal with a group of adults who don't seem to want to participate actively in class discussions and study sessions? Very carefully.

Did you ever watch a young child who was afraid to slide down a playground slide? He probably climbs the ladder, but refuses to let go once he gets to the top. Often a loving parent will climb the ladder with the child, hold him securely in his strong arms, and slide down with the child safely in his grasp. Once the child experiences the fun and excitement, he'll probably race to the ladder and slide down repeatedly.

Adults in Sunday school can be just as insecure as three-year-olds on a slide. Like the wise parent at the playground, the good teacher never forces, demands, humiliates or embarrasses a class member who is hesitant to speak out. He never *ever* violates a person's right *not* to speak. Ordinarily, the skilled group leader does not call on a member by name. Neither does he address a specific question to a specific person. It's easy enough to say something like, "Who knows such and such?" or "Does anyone have any ideas about that?" or "Can any of you tell us something about so and so?" When questions are phrased to avoid putting people on the spot, they might not always be answered, but that's not the most important consideration anyway. A competent teacher is not threatened by a few moments of silence. When the question gets no answer, the leader might simply relax, smile and make a lighthearted comment like "One at a time, please." It's a good idea to have another question ready, but often it only takes re-phrasing the question, an act that accomplishes two purposes: (1) It gives additional time for members to think about the question, and (2) It reassures them that they did understand the question, after all. (What is more embarrassing than answering a question no one asked?)

Like the parent who goes down the slide with the child, a sensitive teacher will do all he can to help class members feel successful. Rather than a response like "No, that's not the right answer," (with "You Dummy" implied), a tactful teacher will offer a reply such as, "What I really had in mind was. . ." In matters of opinion or interpretation, as opposed to factual information, a good response is, "Uhmmm, that's an interesting observation," or "Thanks for adding that. I've never looked at it in that light." It doesn't take a Ph.D. in psychology to learn to encourage rather than intimidate. You can respect a person's right to be there and express his opinions, even if you disagree with him. The teacher is in charge, but not necessarily always right.

This should be especially true in Sunday school, because a Sunday school class should be a support group — a place where individuals care about each other and respect the needs of one another.

After a few successes at group participation, class members will plunge in as eagerly as the kid who discovered the fun of the playground slide.

17

DICK DISCUSS-IT

Unlike most Sunday school teachers, Dick Discuss-It hangs pretty loose. You can frequently hear Dick say, "I don't have to spend much time studying the Sunday school lesson, because we have a lot of discussion. I just throw out an idea, and the group takes it from there." On days when Dick is feeling really spiritual, he reads a verse of scripture and asks class members to tell what it means to them.

Unfortunately, in Dick's class there's a good bit of finger-nail studying, as people endure frequent and prolonged awkward silences. More often there is a great deal of ignorance-pooling. Dick suffers from the misconception that as long as there's talking going on, the class is a walloping success. He hasn't yet figured out that growth and learning are not necessarily taking place when people are talking.

The people who like Dick's class best are those who have an ax to grind. A few folks have found it to be a marvelous platform to air their gripes. One or two of them, usually seize center stage and dominate the discussion. Lots of times people respond to comments without really hearing what has been said, because all they think about during the discussion is what they will say as soon as they get the floor.

In Dick's class, it's frequently either *flight or fight*. There are some members who can't stand a disagreement, so they withdraw or hide their true feelings in order to preserve unity in the group. On the other hand, there are those who think it's not a real discussion unless there's an argument, and they will "take the other side" whether they agree with it or not, just to get a good "fight" going. Consequently, the class usually generates more heat than light.

Because both Dick and the class members never study the lesson and have no learning goals in mind, they often spend the Sunday school hour discussing such topics as the difficulty in finding affordable plumbers, the relative merits of jogging versus running, and the coming sales tax referendum.

Even If Dick Doesn't Do It Right, You Can

Discussion is not just conversation, but it has the purpose of solving a problem, arriving at a decision or coming to an understanding. In Sunday school classes, we most often discuss in order to come to a better understanding of the lesson. An effective discussion provides an opportunity to learn through sharing.

18

BEWARE DISCUSSIONS THAT GENERATE MORE HEAT THAN LIGHT

If you're the teacher of a Sunday school class that uses the discussion method, you can promote more participation by getting rid of the lectern. Don't stand in front of the class like an authority figure. Sit in the circle as a part of the group and choose a different seat every Sunday. If you're always in the same place in the room, class members will begin to see that as the "front of the class," and therefore the authority position.

If you want to be a skillful discussion leader, you'll need to know the material as well as or better than the typical lecturer. You'll ask questions that allow group members to make your points, and then you'll re-state and clarify those points. You'll lead the ideas out of the participants. Be in control of the group, but allow for diversity of opinion and expression.

Prepare more discussion questions than you have time to cover, and always make them *leading* questions. Those are questions that call for thought and that frequently have no simple right or wrong answer. Move the discussion along in an orderly manner by listening, re-phrasing and summarizing the points that have been made and the conclusions that have been

19

reached. In order to do these things, you'll have to spend as much or more time in planning and preparation than you would if you were lecturing. Leading a discussion is *not* the easy way out!

In addition to being prepared yourself, you can help class members prepare in a number of ways. First, see that everyone has a study book, and make sure they know which chapter is coming up next Sunday. Suggest some particular points they might look for as they read the material. Give sneaky little assignments. A sneaky little assignment is one that will stimulate the curiosity of members and leave them eager to learn more. Be sure to make assignments that are not too difficult. Success spawns success, so start with homework that will allow group members to feel they have done well when you call on them next Sunday. *Homework, my foot,* you're thinking. *My class would never do homework for Sunday school!* Don't be so sure. Try this. Call up a few of them early in the week and ask each one to find the answer to a different question. Tell them the answer can be found in the study book or in a particular chapter of the Bible. Ask them to report briefly on it in class. This will give you a head start on a meaningful participation, because several people will have studied the lesson ahead of time, and they'll be dying to show off their knowledge.

In order to guide things along, list on the chalkboard an outline of the areas to be covered that day. The list helps keep the group from getting bogged down. But beware that you don't become a slave to your outline. There's nothing that discourages

DON'T BE A SLAVE TO YOUR LESSON OUTLINE

participation more than making the group feel you don't have time to listen to their questions and comments.

In concluding the discussion, be sure to summarize the main points, mentioning where the group agreed or disagreed, and calling attention to points you need to get back to next week.

BUT WHAT ABOUT THE LECTURE?

There must be something good about the lecture method of teaching Sunday school, because so many people use it. It does provide a way for a large number of people to take advantage of the expertise of a well-qualified teacher, and it does make it possible for the class to stick to the subject (whether they like it or not). But its success is dependent on the personality, speaking ability and knowledge of the lecturer.

The obvious disadvantages of the lecture are that it calls for no advance preparation by the class, it provides no opportunity for group participation and it may not meet the needs or interests of anyone present. Also, who wants to sit through *two* sermons on Sunday morning?

With all its short-comings, there is a place for the lecture, and it can be effective if done well. If you lecture, be sure you can be heard and understood by everyone in the room. Speak slowly and distinctly, smile and keep eye contact with the group. If your eyes are above the door and you drone on in a

IF YOU LECTURE, REMEMBER THAT FEW ADULTS ENJOY BEING READ TO.

21

detached voice, you'll have half the class asleep or planning next week's schedule. Make sure the lighting, ventilation and room temperature are comfortable, or the other half of the class will also be asleep. Know your subject so that you can speak from an outline. Few adults enjoy being read to.

Although the lecture method of teaching allows for minimum group participation, there are a few things you can do to increase interest and involvement: (1) As you progress through the lecture, write essential points on the chalkboard so class members will be more likely to retain those points. (2) In the beginning, ask the group to listen for certain critical points. (3) Ask the class to write out questions that come to them as you lecture, and allow time to deal with these questions. (4) Ask some members to be prepared to summarize the lecture. (5) Ask the class to find reading material for further study of the topic.

Just as there are no perfect teachers, there is also no perfect teaching method. There are advantages and disadvantages to both discussion groups and lecture classes. Frequently it is helpful to use a combination of the methods or to alternate them. But variety for its own sake is ridiculous. Choose the teaching method that is most appropriate to your group and the time available. And if you catch folks snoozing through your class, go back and read this chapter again.

NO TEACHER IS PERFECT

BLUE HAIR IN GRANNY KNOT

SWEATER (CHURCH'S AIR CONDITIONER IS ALWAYS TOO COLD)

ONE SHOULDER PERMANENTLY LOWERED UNDER WEIGHT OF WORLD'S LONGEST SUNDAY SCHOOL PIN

UNIFORM LESSON SERIES LEADER'S GUIDE

KING JAMES VERSION OF THE BIBLE

SUBSTANTIAL CORSET

FRESH HANDKERCHIEF IN PURSE

SENSIBLE SHOES

MISS LILLIE

ANYTHING GOES
FOR DISCUSSION

LOTS OF HAIR
TO LET DOWN

TODAY'S
TOPIC

THE BIG
BANG THEORY

COFFEE
FOR RELAXED
ATMOSPHERE

INFORMAL
ATTIRE TO
PROMOTE
OPENNESS

BIBLE

BIBLE AND
SUNDAY SCHOOL
BOOK (SELDOM USED)

DICK DISCUSS-IT

Rules For Leading A Discussion:

1. Remember that everyone thinks he is the most interesting person alive.
2. With kindness let the group know that "there are no authorities in this class, but I'm in charge here."
3. Do your homework. The leader needs to know at least as much as class members.
4. Sit around a table. It makes you feel more secure to hide your bottom half and have something to lean on.
5. If you can't sit around a table, at least sit in a circle. Allow no one to be on a back row.
6. If there are more than 20 in your group, divide it. Less than 15 is better.
7. Dispel any misconceptions that this is an encounter therapy group or that anyone is reclined on Freud's couch.
8. Make sure everyone understands the topic to be discussed, and then stick to it.
9. Ask questions that allow group members to make the points that you could have made more easily yourself. They need to *say* it more than they need to *hear* it.
10. Learn to *feedback*, i.e., re-phrase what someone said to make sure he, you and others got his point.
11. Remember, it is not necessary to agree, but it is necessary to be civil. After all, you are in a Sunday school class.
12. Never ask a question that can be answered with a simple *yes* or *no*. If you should get that response, ask *why?*
13. Discussion groups are like democracies. Everyone should get an equal chance, so don't let anyone dominate.
14. Tie up loose ends. Summarize main points or decisions the group made.
15. Don't violate a person's right *not* to speak. Don't single out an individual and put him on the spot.
16. Remember, brain and mouth *can* be in gear simultaneously, but it *ain't necessarily so* in every case.

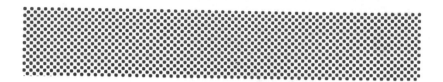

Five Surefire Ways To Kill A Discussion:

1. Ask, "Does anyone have anything to discuss?"
2. Say, "I'm sure you all agree that. . ." (fill in anything here).
3. Ask, "What do you think of sin?"
4. Begin your discussion period with something like the following: "The other night as I was reading from the works of Paul Tillich, as I frequently do, I came across the following statement: 'The confrontation of the existential analysis with the symbol in which Christianity has expressed its ultimate concern is the method which is adequate both to the message of Jesus Christ and to the human predicament as rediscovered in contemporary culture.'[1] What do you think Martin Buber would have to say about this?"
5. Ask any question that can be answered with a simple *yes* or *no*.

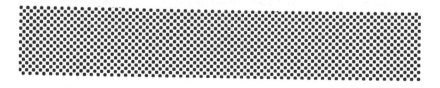

[1]Paul Tillich, *Theology of Culture*, p.49.

What Miss Lillie Could Do (But Probably Won't) To Recharge The Class Battery:

1. Divide the class into buzz groups of six members each and give them six minutes to discuss a topic and then report their findings to the class.
2. Write questions on the chalkboard and let class members vote on which ones to discuss and in what order.
3. Distribute paper and pencils to class members and ask them to write questions they have about the lessons. Then ask class members to volunteer to discuss the questions.
4. Ask two or three class members to role-play a situation suggested by the lesson. (See page 29 for more on role-playing.)
5. Give short, simple assignments to several class members and call on them to make oral reports to the group.
6. Distribute copies of a "test," which class members will take. They do not sign their names. When they complete the "test," they swap papers and discuss the answers.
7. Divide into groups of two or three and paraphrase a brief passage from the Bible or study book.
8. Ask someone (ahead of time) to do a "You Are There" interview related to a Bible character in the lesson or a person who reflects a situation dealt with in the lesson.
9. Brainstorm an idea, topic or question, by asking group members to quickly call out their ideas without regard to how sensible, practical or correct they are. Through this spontaneous contributing of thoughts, you can get a group to open up and follow up later with decisions and conclusions.
10. Ask two or three outgoing, uninhibited members to prepare and present a dramatization that applies to the lesson.
11. Distribute an "opinionnaire," which members can mark and then discuss.

12. Pair off into couples or small groups to share opinions before asking people to speak out and express an opinion to the entire class.

13. Have discussion questions written out on cards to distribute to early arrivals. Ask the first two arrivals to discuss the first question, the next two arrivals the next question, and so on.

14. Ask three or four members to form a panel and discuss a prearranged topic in front of the class. Then allow the class to ask questions of the panel members.

15. Stage a debate between two class members who will prepare information ahead of time and take strong stands on opposite sides of an issue. Then allow the class to ask questions of the debaters.

TRY A ROLE-PLAY

A role-play, unlike a drama, is unrehearsed. There is no script. The role-play is almost spontaneous, in that only a few minutes are allotted for people to think about how the role should be played and what the characters will say.

In a role-play, class members assume the role of characters who have been involved or who might be involved in an actual situation. In "playing the role," a class member can get a better understanding of the issues, and he can better identify with the viewpoint of the person whose role he assumes.

Here are four tips for successful role-playing:

(1)   Keep it brief — no more than ten minutes.

(2)   Let the group structure the role-play, that is, choose the characters and instruct them in how to play the role. (Try not to type-cast!)

(3)   When the "actors" have made the main points clear and the interest is still high, the group leader should cut the scene.

(4)   After the action, the leader should lead the group in a discussion of what took place. Discuss how the role might have been played differently and why.

TRY A ROLE-PLAY

29

Roleplays can be used to make Bible stories come alive, to stimulate discussion on social/ethical issues, and to "get into" any number of situations in which it is useful to emphasize and see other viewpoints.

Here's an example of a roleplay you can try with your class.

THE CLEANSING OF THE TEMPLE

1. Divide the class into two groups. Half the members are scribes, chief priests and temple leaders. The other half are Jesus and his disciples.

2. Both groups should read Matthew 21:12-13, Mark 11:15-19 and Luke 19:45-48.

3. Talk about the episode in the two small groups and discuss points the members feel should be made through the role-play.

4. Each group should select volunteers to assume the roles. Encourage group members to share ideas on how the roles should be played.

5. The "actors" role-play the scene.

6. As a total group, discuss how people felt as they assumed the role of their character. What did they learn from their experience? How do they think the scribes and chief priests felt? Why? How do they think Jesus felt? Why? How do they think the disciples felt? Why? How might the scene have been played differently?

7. The leader should summarize the main points made by the class.

Roleplay situations can be created out of situations quite familiar to the group itself. In devising your role-plays, try to keep the conflict or dilemma well-defined and simple. There are some games that use role-playing as an intregal part of the game. The best of these is the game called, "Can of Squirms"* which is all role-playing. It provides situation dilemmas ("Squirms") selectively chosen to fit a variety of age levels or

Can of Squirms is published by Contemporary Drama Service, a division of Meriwether Publishing Ltd., Box 7710, Colorado Springs, Co 80933

subject areas. There are versions for elementary to college/adult levels as well as special games for both Old and New Testament topics.

HELP IS ON THE WAY

Do you have problems concerning Sunday school? If so, you are not alone. Sunday School Sue will be happy to answer your questions and offer helpful advice. Address your letters to:

**SUNDAY SCHOOL SUE
P.O. BOX 7710
COLORADO SPRINGS, CO 80933**

Following is the first of several excerpts from Sue's wise counsel that you will find throughout this book.

Sunday School Sue

Dear Sue,

I've been a member of the Dorcas Class for 43 years. I've served as card chairman, secretary and hospitality chairman. I'll be perfectly blunt — my feelings have been hurt. You see, in our class we have a sunshine box, which we pass around each week. People contribute money to the sunshine box, and we use these funds to purchase cards and flowers for the sick and bereaved. For example, when our class president had a hysterectomy, they sent her a dozen red roses in a crystal vase. (They only sent me an african violet in a plastic pot when I had gall bladder surgery, but then I was only the card chairman.) Anyway, the class always sends flowers when there is a death in the family of a class member, but they didn't send me so much as a dandelion when my second cousin's mother-in-law passed away recently. What should I do about this?

Short-Changed in Seattle

Dear Short,

Trying to decide who gets flowers and

31

who constitutes "family" is as dangerous as having a beauty contest among children of class members. Take the sunshine box and send it to the starving kids in Ethiopia. Send flowers to no one and cards to everyone. Check with me next spring. I usually have a bumper crop of dandelions, and I'm always happy to share them.

Sunday School Sue

Dear Sunday School Sue:

I've been attending the Men's Bible class in our church for years, and I really enjoy being a part of the group. Sunday school is a good time to visit friends, and we have great hymn-singing before the lesson. My problem is that I just can't manage to stay awake during the lecture. I like the teacher, but he's not the most titillating speaker in the world. About ten minutes into his talk, and I'm zonked out. I have tried every trick I know of to stay awake, but nothing seems to work. Please advise. What should I do? I'm afraid I might be snoring in class.

Drowsy in Denver

Dear Drowsy,

You probably are, but don't worry about it. People have been doing it in church for years. Sorry you don't get more from the lecture, but be thankful for the fellowship you enjoy at Sunday school. That's a legitimate reason to go. Be sure to sit next to a wall and lean against it so you won't fall out of your seat and wake someone else.

Sunday School Sue

Chapter 3:
IT'S WHAT YOU SAY AND NOT JUST HOW YOU SAY IT
The Importance of Content and Curriculum

BARNEY BORN AGAIN

L ike many other Christians, Barney Born Again had a dramatic conversion experience. Naturally it turned his life around, and he is a new creature in the Lord. Barney thinks that unless everyone has a similar conversion experience, which they dwell on as much as he dwells on his, they surely have not *found it.*

With enthusiasm typical of a recent convert, Barney shares his testimony with his Sunday school class every Sunday. Because he is relatively new at teaching Sunday school,

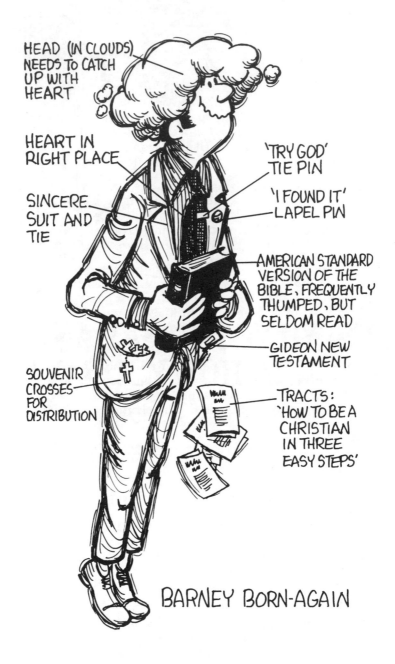

HEAD (IN CLOUDS) NEEDS TO CATCH UP WITH HEART

HEART IN RIGHT PLACE

SINCERE SUIT AND TIE

'TRY GOD' TIE PIN

'I FOUND IT' LAPEL PIN

AMERICAN STANDARD VERSION OF THE BIBLE, FREQUENTLY THUMPED, BUT SELDOM READ

GIDEON NEW TESTAMENT

SOUVENIR CROSSES FOR DISTRIBUTION

TRACTS: 'HOW TO BE A CHRISTIAN IN THREE EASY STEPS'

BARNEY BORN-AGAIN

he knows little or nothing about curriculum materials. He has never heard testimony about the conversion experience of curriculum writers, so he doesn't put much stock in anything they have to offer.

Barney Born Again is convinced that the Bible is God's word, although he has just barely begun to read it. (He started with the book of John, which he is halfway through.) Originally he had intended to teach the Bible, the whole Bible, and nothing but the Bible. However, he's beginning to get bogged down in John, so for several Sundays he's taught from a pamphlet distributed by a non-denominational organization that explains how to live the Christian life in three easy steps.

Barney, with all his good intentions and sincerity is often guilty of what big-time theologians call *eisegesis*. In other words, he picks a verse of scripture and decides what it means to him, putting his own meaning into it, rather than seeking to know what the writer was really trying to say in the passage.

Few of Barney's class members have shared their conversion experiences with him, so Barney assumes they are not privy to all the spiritual secrets he enjoys. It has never entered his mind that other people might know as much or more than he knows about living the Christian life.

Barney spends very little time studying to prepare for his Sunday school class. He depends on the Holy Spirit to speak to him and tell him what to say. It has not yet occurred to Barney that one of these days the Holy Spirit might say, "Barney, old boy, you're unprepared. You should have studied the Bible, the commentary, the lesson book, and the teacher's guide."

GLENDA GURU

She makes you laugh. She makes you cry. She holds the group in the palm of her hand with tales so emotional and personal you can't help but identify with her. Glenda Guru knows how to play on every emotion you possess, and she does it with charm and wit.

This popular speaker is attractive, articulate and exhibitionist enough to relate family secrets every Sunday morning. One minute she spellbinds her audience with tear-jerking accounts of her son's arduous recovery from drug addiction or her grandmother's battle with cancer, and the next minute she has everyone in stitches with the latest joke.

Glenda not only has an abundant supply of humorous anecdotes available for quick recall, she has a wealth of life experience to share. She's done or had it all. She delights in describing the traumas of her husband's early business failure, her daughter's divorce, and her own hysterectomy.

Glenda is presently the teacher of an adult Sunday school class, but no one would be surprised if she soon became the stand-in for a TV talk show personality, or at least a co-host for next year's Academy Awards, because her ability to entertain and inspire are unparalleled.

In addition to having an effervescent personality and a joke for every occasion, Glenda seems to have a private pipeline to the Lord. She can tell you in great detail how The Man Upstairs miraculously healed her from a rare and incurable disease, repaired her dishwasher, and found her a parking space when she was late for the duplicate bridge tournament.

Glenda is a fine Christian. She's talented, energetic and well meaning. But she's like most of us in that her favorite subject is herself, and that's the main topic of her teaching. Her lesson content, in various guises is "What the Lord has done for me, and what I've done for the Lord." There are some good points and many elements of truth in Glenda's teaching, but frequently she reduces answers to life's complex problems to a simple A.B.C. formula

Like the Pied Piper, Glenda has a faithful following of regulars who wouldn't miss her Sunday morning hour of inspiration and entertainment. The class is centered around the personality of the teacher, and if Glenda gave up the class, some of the class members would give up Sunday school.

Some members of her class have become disillusioned and

GLENDA GURU

have dropped out of Sunday school. They began to feel that their intelligence was a bit insulted by Glenda's approach, and they recognized the limitations of Glenda's teaching. One class dropout was heard to say, "Hey man, everyone has personal, family and health problems. I'm glad the Lord helped Glenda with hers, but I'm tired of hearing about them. And besides, when I want to hear a comedy routine, I'll turn on my TV."

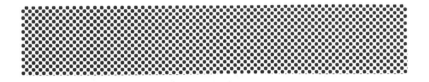

Subjects Not To Belabor In Sunday School:

1. Your surgery
2. Your spouse's surgery
3. Your relative's surgery
4. Your neighbor's surgery
5. Your marital problems, past or present
6. Your financial problems, past or present
7. Your in-law problems, past or present
8. Your conversion experience
9. Your wicked past
10. Your dog's surgery

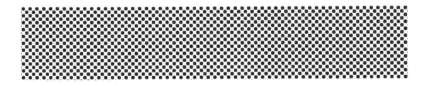

CARLTON CLIPPER

If Carlton Clipper ever loses his scissors, he'll suffer withdrawal severe enough to require a padded cell. Carlton is an avid reader — of everything but the Bible and the Sunday school book.

Carlton clips out columns by Billy Graham, Ann Landers, William Buckley and George Will to share with his adult Sunday school class every Sunday. Sometimes there are stories from *Readers Digest* that he brings to read, and frequently there's an essay from *Time* magazine that he feels is worth sharing.

It makes no difference what the scheduled lesson is about, Carlton will depart from it in order to read an article he found during the week that grabbed his attention. He never summarizes the content of the material or uses it as a springboard for discussion. He just reads it.

There seems to be no rhyme or reason that determines what type of material Carlton reads. Usually the information is worthwhile, and sometimes it has an inspiring message. But often the reading selections of this inveterate clipper simply reflect and reinforce his personal and political views and have little or no relationship to the class members' need to learn and grow as Christian disciples.

Recently Carlton discovered that his church has a tape library, so sometimes instead of reading to his class, he brings a tape recorder to Sunday school and lets the class listen to some recorded words of inspiration or instruction.

Carlton was very impressed with the book, *Two From Galilee* by Marjorie Holmes, so he plans to read it aloud in installments — a chapter a Sunday — for the next several months in his Sunday school class.

Not surprisingly, Carlton's class has been dwindling in numbers lately. Those few who are left are considering breaking the news to Carlton that they too went to school, and although some are more proficient at it than others, every person in the class can read. Some have even thought of hiding Carlton's scissors.

EAR TUNED FOR
USABLE QUOTES

PERPETUAL MOTION
SCISSORS

VARIOUS
10-YEAR
SUBSCRIPTIONS

POSSIBLY
A BIBLE

CARLTON CLIPPER

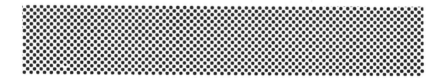

Excellent Publications That Are Not Sunday School Books:

1. Readers Digest
2. Time
3. U.S. News and World Report
4. Newsweek
5. National Geographic
6. Guideposts
7. Christian Herald
8. Moody Monthly
9. The Saturday Evening Post
10. People Weekly

CONTENT AND CURRICULUM

Barney Born Again, Glenda Guru and Carlton Clipper have worlds of talent, Christian dedication, reading skills, leadership ability and personal charisma among them. They could be fantastic Sunday school teachers.

What they need (among other things) is a fundamental understanding of the importance of a sound curriculum in Sunday school. If their teaching is to make a difference to their students, helping them to live the Christian life each day, these teachers must have content, direction and comprehensiveness in their lessons. They could find these in a good Sunday school curriculum.

Sunday school leaders have realized the need for adequate curriculum materials from the earliest days of the Sunday school movement. The American Uniform Lessons were printed as early as 1826, and by 1872, Sunday schoolers all across the country were studying the same lessons in the Uniform Lesson series. Curriculum materials have continued to improve over the years.

Since those first lessons were published, denominational and commercial publishing houses have produced gigantic amounts of curriculum resources for churches, and most of these materials are targeted at the Sunday school.

Where to Look for Curriculum Materials

While there are some excellent curriculum resources available through interdenominational and non-denominational publishing companies, you are always safe in looking first to your own denomination's publishing house for Sunday school literature.

Curriculum materials are generally prepared and authorized as official products of the denomination. They are based on and undergirded by the theological position and doctrinal emphasis of the particular church. Denominations try to interpret theological insights and mission programs through their teaching materials. Those who write curriculum resources do so under careful supervision,. These people are usually the church's most competent, dedicated Christian educators and scholars.

Curriculum is More Than Printed Matter

Printed Sunday school books and other resource materials

FIRST PICK MATERIALS FROM YOUR OWN DENOMINATION

are vital parts of a church's Christian education curriculum, but curriculum is not limited to printed matter. It is more than a course of study, more than biblical knowledge, more than memorized doctrinal statementss, more than conformity to ethical standards.

The Sunday school curriculum is whatever the Sunday school does to achieve its purpose. It is the living experience of persons in Christian fellowship as they come to know God, grow in their relationship to him and seek to understand and do his will under the direction of Christian teachers.

The Sunday school curriculum includes programs, literature, activities and efforts to provide an atmosphere of revelation and response between people and God and a climate for growth in Christian discipleship. Methods used in implementing curriculum must be determined by the nature of the Christian message. In other words, the Sunday school teaches not only by what it says, but by what it does. Children, youth and adults are sensitivie to their atmosphere.

Characteristics of Good Curriculum Materials

A good curriculum is carefully planned and designed with a specific purpose in mind. The objective of the printed Sunday school literature is the same as the objective of the church's educational ministry. Each unit of study is planned and pre-

44

GOOD CURRICULUM HAS A SPECIFIC PURPOSE

sented in the light of that objective.

The overall plan of a good curriculum allows for various ages and stages of development in Christian maturity, awareness and response. Materials provide for progression and at the same time are aimed at a person's need at a given age. A good curriculum reflects the understanding that the Christian experience is a process of becoming, so we can both achieve objectives and still be working toward them.

A good curriculum is both person-centered and Bible-centered. That is to say it recognizes the needs of individuals and seeks to meet people where they are in their personal and Christian development. At the same time, it has as its foundation the message of the Bible and seeks to teach that message in a meaningful way. A good curriculum is rich in content, sound in educational principles and tasteful in style and content.

How to Use Curriculum Materials

We get the cart before the horse if we are more concerned with covering the lesson than with the needs of the learner. What happens to the curriculum materials is not as important as what happens to the people for whom the literature is intended. The effective teacher remembers that resources are tools to be used in providing experiences of Christian growth, not ends in themselves.

45

CAUTION: CURRICULUM RESOURCES CAN BE USED TOO CREATIVELY.

The material consumed is more important than the material covered. It is better to have a close encounter with a small amount of material than to have a whole lesson just thrown at the class.

Nearly all Sunday school books come with a teacher's guide. The teacher's guide is to teaching as a recipe is to cooking. Don't wait until you ruin the dinner to read the directions.

Because Sunday school curriculum resources are means and not ends, they should be used creatively. But don't adapt so freely that you defeat the plans within the curriculum for comprehensiveness and progression in Christian education.

Resources cannot do the job alone. Good Sunday school literature does not necessarily guarantee good teaching, but a sound curriculum carefully used can help in achieving the purpose of the Sunday school teacher. Christian education does not usually rise above the level of the printed materials used.

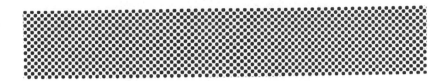

How To Learn To Be A Sunday School Teacher:

1. Study at an accredited college for a bachelor's degree in liberal arts.
2. Also, attend a certified seminary for a master's degree in Christian education.
3. Also, attend week-long lab schools and training workshops each summer at your church's conference grounds.
4. Also, attend week-end leadership education seminars in nearby towns.
5. Also, observe other teachers for on-the-job training.
6. Also, read all the books listed on page 53.
7. Also, earn a doctorate degree in theology.
8. Also, go through psycho-analysis in order to understand yourself and others.
9. Also, have thirty years' practical experience as a teacher.
10. Or — if time and money do not allow the above — simply read the directions in the teacher's guide that accompanies your Sunday school literature.

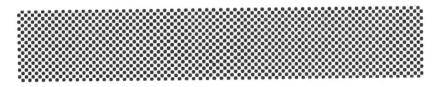

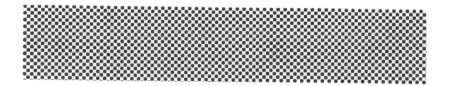

Some Creative Uses For The Teacher's Guide:

1. Stack up several for your four-year-old to sit on so he can reach the table.
2. Slide a couple under the leg of that wobbly table in order to level it.
3. Open and hold over your head when it's raining and you have no hat or umbrella.
4. Read it at the hair dresser's or in any waiting area. People will be struck by your spirituality.
5. Box up several dozen and send to missionaries in Shri Lanka. (Never mind that Shri Lankans don't read English. They can use them to level wobbly tables.)
6. Tie securely in bundles of a dozen and use as door stops.
7. Chink windows with them in January for increased energy efficiency.
8. Donate them to the Scouts for their paper drive.
9. Use for a fan in church when the air conditioner is on the blink.
10. If all else fails, try reading carefully, following directions, and using as a guide for your Sunday school lesson. You'll be amazed at its usefulness.

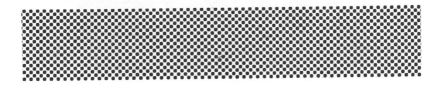

Subjects You Can Get People to Speak On if You're A Lazy Sunday School Teacher:

1. Community Beautification
2. C.P.R. Can Save Your Life
3. American Cancer Society film, "Breast Self-Examination"
4. Fund Raising for Democrats or Republicans
5. PTA Membership Drive
6. Your Volunteer Fire Department Needs You
7. Needlepoint for All Ages
8. Fun With Weight Watchers
9. The United Way Campaign
10. Macro-biotic Recipes for Health and Happiness

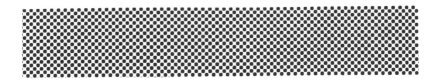

You will find volunteers throughout your community eager to speak to any assembled group on these and a variety of other interesting topics totally unsuited to Sunday school.

Sunday School Sue

Dear Sunday School Sue,

I teach a children's class in Sunday school. The suggestions in the literature for class activities are things that take extra materials and a lot of preparation, and I don't have much time to devote to getting the supplies gathered together and ready every Sunday morning. The student's book contains simple stories about children's problems. These kids are too big for stories. Sometimes we have a unit on church history or Bible study, and that bores the class to death.

Why can't we have something that is easier on the teacher? Please excuse me for complaining, but I hate the literature. What do you suggest?

Frustrated in Phoenix

Dear Frustrated,

Don't apologize for complaining about the Sunday school literature. People have been complaining about it as long as kids have complained about school lunches. People will continue to complain about it as long as people complain about their in-laws.

Before you start looking for new literature, try planning ahead and see if you can do some of those activities that require advanced preparation. Go through the entire unit and make a list of needed supplies and resources. Keep the list with you, and you'll be surprised how much you can pick up when you're at the church or the store for some other reason.

Also, try studying your Sunday school lesson on Sunday afternoon — a whole week before the next lesson. When you have

all week to think about it, you'll see that some of those activities are not as impossible as you had imagined.

If you are using literature that is part of a soundly planned curriculum, there is a reason for the stories and activities that are included. They are part of a bigger picture based on the developmental needs of the kids.

Be creative with the literature. Curriculum materials are like hot dogs. Sometimes people eat them plain, and sometimes they need to add a variety of condiments. But don't be so creative that you lose the weiner and the bun.

Try to follow directions more closely, plan ahead and be creative. If that doesn't work, talk to your minister about the curriculum. (I sound like Ann Landers, don't I?) He can tell you if it is the best your denomination has to offer. If it's not, order the best.

Sunday School Sue

How to Prepare for a Sunday School Lesson

1. **Begin early.** Sunday afternoon the week before is a good time.
2. **Pray about it.** It's amazing what can be accomplished through ordinary, garden variety people when there's guidance from above.
3. **Read the lesson** in both the student's book and teacher's book.
4. **Think about the PURPOSE of the lesson.** Do you really understand what it is? What is the lesson supposed to accomplish?
5. **Read the lesson's Bible passage** in several translations. Look up words or ideas you aren't familiar with in a commentary or Bible dictionary.
6. **Re-read student's book and teacher's book.**
7. **Decide how YOU think the lesson should be approached.** Develop your own tailor-made lesson plan with your own particular class in mind.
8. **Outline lesson plan,** including activities for the session.
9. **Gather needed resources,** supplemental materials and supplies.
10. **Go to the church Friday or Saturday or VERY EARLY Sunday morning** and get the room ready.

BEGIN EARLY
TO PREPARE
NEXT SUNDAY'S
LESSON

HELPFUL BOOKS FOR
SUNDAY SCHOOL TEACHERS

Basic Skills for Church Teachers by Donald L. Griggs, *Abingdon*

Exploring the Bible With Children by Dorothy Jean Furnish, *Abingdon*

The Joy of Teaching by Beth A. Bowser, *Discipleship Resources*

Learning Together in Christian Fellowship by Sara Little, *John Knox Press*

Planning for Teaching Church School by Donald L. Griggs, *Judson*

Teaching as Jesus Taught by Georgianna Summers, *Discipleship Resources*

The Way of the Teacher by Donald B. Rogers

Order above books from:

Discipleship Resources
P.O. Box 189
Nashville, TN 37202

Celebrating Special Days in the Church School Year by Judy Gattis Smith, *Meriwether Publishing, Ltd.*

Order above book from:

Meriwether Publishing, Ltd.
P.O. Box 7710
Colorado Springs, Co 80933

FOOD FOR THOUGHT

What does a Sunday school teacher teach? "Why Sunday school, you dummy," is one possible answer to that question. Some other answers are:

1. *The Sunday school teacher teaches people.*
2. *The Sunday school teacher teaches the Bible.*
3. *The Sunday school teacher teaches the lesson in the Sunday school book.*
4. *The Sunday school teacher teaches the Gospel.*
5. *The Sunday school teacher teaches Christian faith and discipleship.*

What is your answer?

Which would you rather use in teaching Sunday school, a lesson that is centered on the Bible or one that is centered on the needs of the individual? Which would you consider more helpful, an experience-centered curriculum or a content-centered curriculum?

Which is more dangerous, the pursuit of knowledge for its own sake, or the idea that it doesn't matter what we believe as long as we're sincere?

If you can't decide on answers to these questions, don't feel like the Lone Ranger. If you're thinking about these questions, you're on the right track.

THEOLOGY IN SUNDAY SCHOOL

"Don't confuse me with theology, just give me a Sunday school lesson that teaches the Bible." Sorry, kiddo. You're out of luck. Asking for a Sunday school lesson without theology is like asking for a dry ocean.

Theology is the truth about God in relationship to mankind. (Go back and read that last sentence again.) What we believe about God and his relationship to individuals determines our motives, our goals, our methods and our procedures in Sunday school. (Please think about that last statement for the next several hours.)

What we believe about the nature of God and the nature of human beings and the relationship of the two determines how we interpret the Bible. And don't say, "Just tell me what the Bible says, don't interpret it," because you'd have as much success in finding a dry ocean as in reading the Bible without interpreting it. You cannot ask what the Bible says without also asking what the Bible means, and to ask what it means is to interpret it.

YOU CAN'T ASK WHAT THE BIBLE SAYS WITHOUT ASKING WHAT THE BIBLE MEANS

If all of this is getting too sticky, just remember that we have dedicated Christian scholars who devoted years of thorough, disciplined study to these complexities. Many of them are the writers of Sunday school curriculum materials.

Assuming you want the theological basis of your Sunday school lessons to agree with that of your denomination, count on the curriculum writers of your church's publishing house to keep you on the right track.

If you don't like what your denomination is publishing, you probably need more study on the subject, or perhaps you should check out the church down the street.

Chapter 4:
THE CARE, FEEDING, MOTIVATION, AND MAINTENANCE OF SUNDAY SCHOOL TEACHERS

SENATOR UPSOME

Fifteen years ago Senator Upsome volunteered to teach the Men's Bible Class. That was about six months before he ran for his first public office, a seat on the local Board of Education.

At that time, Senator Upsome had already come up some in the world. He had come up some financially as a result of sharp business acumen and shrewd deals. He had also come up some socially by marrying a doctor's daughter and moving to the best neighborhood.

DETERMINATION, ENTHUSIASM, IMAGINATION, HARD WORK... THEY SUCCEED IN POLITICS, BUSINESS AND IN SUNDAY SCHOOL

SCAR TISSUE

15-YEAR PIN

NOW PRESSED FOR TIME, BUT STILL A DEDICATED TEACHER

EXCELLENT AND INCREASING KNOWLEDGE OF THE BIBLE

SENATOR UPSOME

There were people in town who thought that Upsome was trying to gain respectability and popularity and come up some more by teaching the prestigious Men's Bible Class. A few even suggested to the preacher that Upsome's motives had more to do with image building or business and political contacts than with a desire to teach religious truth.

But the preacher calmly replied, "Let him who always has pure motives cast the first stone. And besides, no one else is willing to take the class."

Upsome worked closely with the preacher, grateful for the study books and helpful resources the preacher provided him. The optimistic minister thought to himself, "Ours is not to reason why; ours is but to help him try."

And try he did. Upsome met the challenge of the Men's Bible Class with the same determination, enthusiasm and hard work that accounted for his success in business and politics. The preacher said it was a miracle what the Lord could do with folks who were willing. Upsome, the preacher and the Lord stuck it out with each other, and by the time Upsome had been elected senator, he had an impressive knowledge of the Bible, which he shared skillfully with the fellows in the Men's Bible Class. Both Upsome and other class members came up some spiritually as well.

MOTIVATIONS OF SUNDAY SCHOOL TEACHERS

If all Sunday school teachers waited until they were completely qualified to handle the job before they attempted to teach a class, the Sunday school would have gone belly-up over a century ago.

When asked to teach a class, most people immediately think of a number of reasons to decline the invitation. Nobody feels qualified or good enough. We all think we don't have a strong enough faith or sufficient knowledge or the necessary skills and ability to work with people.

Fortunately, perfection has never been a prerequisite for the position. Even Jesus picked some obviously imperfect folks to handle the task of establishing the early church, and they managed to get the job done by remembering that their teacher had said, "Lo, I am with you always."

Few people decide to teach Sunday school because they feel qualified. Most do so for a number of other reasons. Some may accept the responsibility out of a sense of gratitude for those who have taught them the Christian faith — their own former Sunday school teachers, ministers, parents and friends who helped shape their lives by showing them the ways of Christ.

Some decide to teach Sunday school in order to learn more of the Bible and the Christian life. They realize that the teacher learns and grows more than anyone else in the class, at the same time helping others to learn and grow.

There are those who teach Sunday school because of a sense that God needs their talents and time in his service. They feel an obligation to serve their church and help fill its needs.

There may even be some who choose to teach a Sunday school class for the wrong reasons. Human motivations are as complex as the human personality. When a person takes on the job of Sunday school teacher, for whatever reason, he or she greatly increases the possibility of growth in religious knowledge, grace and the love of God.

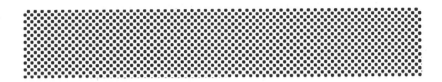

Some Other Reasons People Teach Sunday School:

We asked a thousand Sunday school teachers why they agreed to teach their class. Those who wish to remain anonymous answered as follows:

1. *"I didn't have the nerve to tell the preacher no. He makes me feel guilty anyway."*
2. *"I guess it's my time. Everybody ought to do it sooner or later."*
3. *"I thought they'd never ask. It gave me a great opportunity to escape that boring adult class I was in."*
4. *"Teaching Sunday school will enhance my personal respectability and reputation in the community."*
5. *"It will be a nice addition to the eulogy at my funeral."*
6. *"There will be many stars in my crown by and by."*
7. *"I wanted to prove to my mother-in-law that I did amount to something."*
8. *"They said they were desperate."*
9. *"It will force me to come to Sunday school."*
10. *"It will give me a great chance to straighten out some people."*

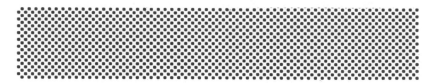

Who Me? Teach Sunday School? You Gotta Be Kidding!

A recent survey among those who graciously declined the invitation to teach Sunday school revealed the following reasons they turned down the offer.

1. *"I'm not qualified. Kids are too smart these days."*
2. *"I'm too young. Sunday school teachers are supposed to be extremely mature — say about 95."*
3. *"I'm too old. I've done my share. I kept the nursery in 1958 and worked with those hippie kids in the 60's. Let someone else do it."*
4. *"I'm too busy. I work all week and have meetings lots of nights."*
5. *"The pay is lousy."*
6. *"Kids make me nervous, and I don't know enough to teach adults."*
7. *"We have season tickets to the University ball games, and we usually spend the night."*
8. *"My bursitis flares up in bad weather."*
9. *"I don't have any sensible shoes. Aren't Sunday school teachers supposed to wear sensible shoes?"*
10. *"In a church this size there should be plenty of other people to do it."*

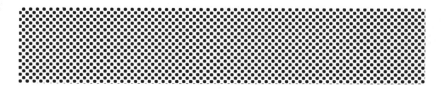

HOW TO ENCOURAGE PEOPLE
TO TEACH SUNDAY SCHOOL

Ever heard this story? Some poor, unsuspecting fellow with all the good intentions in the world and absolutely no teaching experience agrees to teach the seventh graders in Sunday school. Someone hands him a quarterly and points him in the direction of the classroom.

The person who was in charge of teacher recruitment is delighted to have the slot filled. He had been turned down by a dozen people before he finally found the fellow who said yes. So great is the relief of the recruiter that he promptly forgets the matter and goes on to other concerns.

The new teacher does his best to deal effectively with the kids, but he had forgotten how obstreperous 12- and 13-year-olds can be. Soon he feels he is a total failure as a Sunday school teacher. He realizes the kids are uncooperative because they are uninterested, but he doesn't know what to do about it. He decides he's incapable of teaching, and he blames his failure on his own imagined personality defects.

No one offers him any help. He has no idea that there are additional resources he could use, much less where he would find them. When he has a legitimate reason for being absent from Sunday school, he has no one to call on to substitute for him.

63

The teacher becomes more and more frustrated with every disastrous Sunday. After several months, he gives up, vowing never to teach Sunday school again, and hoping never to encounter another seventh grader as long as he lives.

The recruiter starts all over again begging church members to take the seventh grade class, but no one wants to do it because by this time the seventh graders have the reputation of always driving their teachers nuts.

There Is Another way

There are several things that could have been done differently to make the story have a happy ending. First, a prospective teacher should be given the opportunity to observe several class sessions before he or she agrees to take on the job. People need to know what they're getting into. (You're thinking they might be scared off, and you're right, but after all if there's going to be honesty anywhere, it should be in Sunday school.)

Prospective teachers should be given a written job outline explaining exactly what is expected of them. They should not be told how easy the job will be.

No teacher should be asked to take a class indefinitely. One year is a good length of time for most people. At the end of that year, the teacher should be replaced if he or she wishes to be. A lot more people would teach if they knew they could count on not being stuck with the class for a lifetime.

Every Sunday school teacher should be supplied with a reliable substitute when there is a legitimate reason for absence. Of course teachers should respect the schedules of substitutes and not call on them at the last minute except in cases of dire emergency.

Good literature and supplemental resources are available by the truckloads, but most teachers don't know about them. Someone must see to it that teachers find out about what is available. Someone must also see that this material is ordered and distributed promptly.

Frequently Sunday school teachers need more equipment or supplies in their classrooms. This could be anything from chalk to chairs. Volunteers should not have to beg for basic teaching equipment. Someone should ask the teacher what is needed and see that it is made available. Usually it's not lack of money but lack of communication that causes Sunday school classrooms to be poorly furnished and equipped.

Religious publishing houses turn out scores of how-to-books that would be helpful to Sunday school teachers. Most denominations print pamphlets and booklets with valuable information on how to improve teaching skills. Somebody needs to see that teachers see these.

It always helps to have someone to talk to about problems or successes. The support of the minister or a church staff member can be vital to a struggling teacher who needs a shoulder to cry on or a word of encouragement. Meetings with other teachers from time to time to discuss common concerns can be invaluable.

Whenever possible, churches should foot the bill for teacher training seminars or workshops. It's an extremely worthwhile investment. Sometimes teachers would attend such training sessions if they had help with child care or transportation.

More people would probably teach Sunday school if more recognition and appreciation for their efforts were shown. Sunday school teachers deserve a lot of credit for their faithfulness. It's a sin and shame to make them feel guilty and inept like the poor guy who failed so miserably with the seventh graders. He should have been a success.

MORE PEOPLE WOULD TEACH IF THEY WERE
GIVEN RECOGNITION AND APPRECIATION

MAINTAINING ENTHUSIASM

Keeping romance alive is not the only thing that takes thought, work and creativity. Maintaining interest and enthusiasm for teaching a Sunday school class every week does too. There are several things teachers can do to avoid burn-out.

Plan ahead and you won't fall into the panic trap. Self-confidence is markedly increased when adequate preparation has been made, and as self-confidence blossoms, teaching becomes a joy, not a chore.

Avoid going "stale" by staying out of a rut. Vary your lesson plan and procedures from week to week, and both you and your students will find the class more interesting. Be brave as you try new and different approaches. Keep the class wondering what you will do next. Predictability can be the kiss of death. Stand on your head and whistle "Dixie" if it takes it.

Keep the room as attractive as possible. Rearrange the chairs. Change the bulletin board. Put up some new pictures. Put a vase of flowers in the window sill. Put a tablecloth on that tacky old table in the corner. Enlist class members to get involved in sprucing up the room. They'll probably be glad to volunteer touches of brightness.

In nice weather let the class meet outdoors every now and then. This of course is especially effective if you're studying nature and the marvels of God's creation.

Surprise your class with juice and cookies two or three times a year. Be sure they know that you provided that treat in appreciation for them because they are the very best class in all the world, and you love every one of them dearly.

Get class members to help you teach. Even if your class is composed of young children, you can give them some simple assignment to assist with the lesson. Ask them to look up a Bible verse or bring in a pretty colored fall leaf or find a picture in a magazine that applies to the lesson. Naturally, youth and adults can be given more involved assignments. Make them feel they are really helping and not doing meaningless busy work. Make sure all assignments can be accomplished with success by the students. Nobody wants to fail at anything.

If you are a teacher of children or youth, don't stay in your teaching position too long. Go back into an adult class after two or three years. The fellowship, knowledge and inspiration available there will enable you to be a better teacher when the time comes to return to a teaching position. Or on the other hand, the adult class might be so boring that you'll be chomping at the bit to get back to teaching kids.

It needs to be said again — enthusiasm is contagious. When your class sees that you think Sunday school is interesting, fun, important, worthwhile and a place for pleasant surprises, they'll be likely to share your feelings.

As your students become more enthusiastic about Sunday school, so will you. Cycles are not always vicious.

ENTHUSIASM IS CONTAGIOUS

HOW TO SHOW APPRECIATION FOR SUNDAY SCHOOL TEACHERS

RULE No.1: DON'T ASK TEACHERS TO HELP WITH THE DINNER

Appreciation for the efforts of Sunday school teachers should be expressed frequently and sincerely, not only by the minister or church staff person, but by class members as well. Here are some ways to honor teachers.

If your church has a Sunday School Teacher Appreciation Banquet, don't let any Sunday school teachers bring food, set tables or serve on the clean-up committee. If you must, get the local taco establishment to cater the affair, just don't let the teachers do a thing. That's rule number one.

Get a church member who is good with photography to visit Sunday school classes and take candid shots of the teachers at work. Then add catchy captions to the photos and decorate a bulletin board with them.

Select a "Teacher of the Month," and put a large photo of that person on the bulletin board. Include interesting information about the teacher's background, hobbies, family and career.

Have a "Feature Teacher" each week in the church bulletin or newsletter. Write a paragraph about the teacher and his or her class. Include words of appreciation for specific things the teacher has accomplished.

All teachers should receive a letter from the minister or church educational worker at least once a year expressing gratitude for their time and effort. A phone call asking if there are any problems or needs wouldn't hurt.

The minister should mention Sunday school teachers and other church workers frequently in his pastoral prayer during the Sunday morning worship service. All church members should be encouraged to pray regularly for Sunday school teachers.

Someone who is handy with a video camera, could make a video of Sunday school teachers in action. All teachers could be interviewed and asked about their teaching methods, the curriculum materials they use, what they like about teaching, what has been most meaningful to them, etc. The video could be shown at a church fellowship supper or on Christian Education Sunday. If the video is not practical, try a slide presentation.

On Christian Education Sunday every teacher could be given a corsage or boutonniere to wear to church.

The names of all Sunday school teachers along with the class they teach should be listed in the church bulletin and/or newsletter annually.

A service of dedication should be held once a year during the morning worship hour. At that time all Sunday school teachers should be introduced and "installed." A momento such as a certificate, teacher's pin, or devotional book could be presented to teachers as a token of appreciation.

Perhaps following the dedication service or at another appropriate time, a reception could be held in honor of Sunday school teachers. Rule number one applies here also.

Above all, every Sunday school teacher in the world should be presented with a copy of THE OFFICIAL SUNDAY SCHOOL TEACHERS HANDBOOK.

Sunday School Sue

Dear Sunday School Sue,

I have a terrible problem that's keeping me from attending Sunday school. Our church has some people who smoke, drink, gossip, tell little white lies and run around. I'm sure some of them are deacons, so I'll bet some are also Sunday school teachers. What should I do about all those hypocrites.?

Agitated in Akron

Dear Agitated,

You're absolutely right. You do have a terrible problem. Run — don't walk to the church and get involved in as many aspects of the church's program as you possibly can, including Sunday school. One of two things is sure to happen. Either your advanced spirituality and superior holiness will rub off on some of those awful hypocrites, or you will see that those folks are regular human beings with shortcomings they are trying to overcome. Be sure and discuss the problem with God, but don't mention it to anyone else.

Sunday School Sue

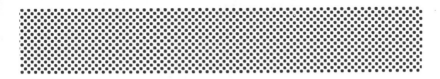

The Best Sunday School Teacher*

More than 1,000 people told what they value in their teacher:

1. Loves and is concerned about persons
2. Is well versed in the Bible and Christian beliefs
3. Encourages the group to discuss the issues
4. Gives evidence of his or her own faith
5. Is sincere
6. Uses good teaching methods
7. Is a good speaker
8. Knows those in his or her group personally

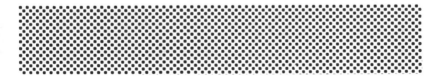

*(By Warren Hartman, Board of Discipleship from the PEOPLE TO PEOPLE tabloid, page 7, Fall, 1985. Copyright 1985 by Graded Press. Used by permission.)

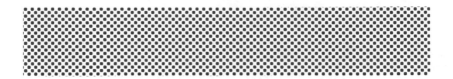

What Frustrates Sunday School Teachers:

1. Late arrivals.
2. Early departures (usually for choir practice).
3. People popping in to make announcements.
4. Groups who use the classroom during the week and don't leave it as they found it.
5. The chalk monster.

What A Sunday School Teacher Likes To Hear:

1. Thank you very much.
2. Keep up the good work.
3. See you next Sunday.
4. I enjoyed the lesson.
5. Would you like to have dinner with our family next Sunday?

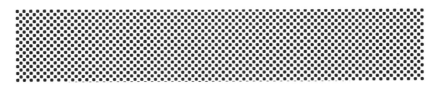

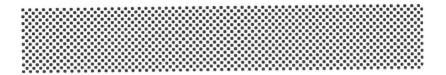

What Should Be Expected Of A Sunday School Teacher?

1. Prepare the lesson for each class session.
2. Get there on time (several minutes before students).
3. Set a good example in personal life.
4. Give advance notice if substitute is needed.
5. Have a willingness to learn, grow, stretch.
6. Use the denomination's recommended curriculum resources.
7. Get to know members of the class and their needs and abilities.
8. Get the room ready ahead of time.
9. Participate in available training opportunities.
10. Participate in worship and other areas of church life.

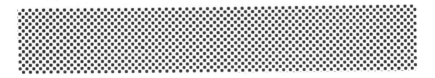

What A Sunday School Teacher Should Expect Of The Church:

1. Chalk.
2. Quality literature in sufficient quantity for the class.
3. Adequate room for teaching.
4. Necessary teaching equipment and furnishings.
5. Opportunities for training and further education.
6. A description of what is expected of him or her.
7. Limited tenure.
8. Substitutes when needed.
9. Support of the minister and church staff.
10. Chalk.

THE CHALK MONSTER

Times People Want To See Their Sunday School Teacher:

1. When they are taking a basket to a needy family.
2. When they're taking the kids to see a G rated movie.
3. At P.T.A.
4. While helping a little old lady across the street.
5. While checking out inspirational books from the library.
6. While visiting at the nursing home.
7. When buying Girl Scout cookies.
8. When coming out of the voting booth.

Times When People Don't Want To See Their Sunday School Teacher:

1. When they are trying to fix a traffic ticket.
2. When they burned a finger and uttered a four-letter word.
3. When dealing with an insurance claims adjuster.
4. At R rated movies.
5. When they are mowing the lawn at 10:00 a.m. on Sunday.
6. During an I.R.S. audit.
7. When bets are being taken at the office football pool.
8. At the liquor store.

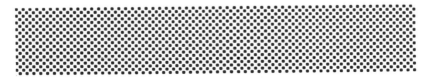

THE LIFESTYLE OF A
SUNDAY SCHOOL TEACHER

There are a few things that are unique to the lifestyle of Sunday school teachers, among them diet, exercise and sex life.

Sunday School Teacher's Diet:

This diet will do nothing for weight control or nutrition, but it will supply the Sunday school teacher with a world of supplies for craft time.

A dozen popsicles daily. *(Use popsicle sticks to make baskets, miniature cabins, etc.)*

A dozen eggs daily. *(Use cartons to make trash cans. Save eggshells for mosaics.)*

One carrot daily. *(Grow carrot tops in a saucer in the window sill of the classroom.)*

One potato daily. *(Grow potato vines next to carrot tops.)*

A can of anything daily. *(Make pencil holders from cans.)*

A tub of margarine daily. *(Make flower pots from tubs.)*

A box of oatmeal daily. *(Make drums from oatmeal boxes.)*

Whatever punch and animal crackers are left over if you teach preschoolers. Whatever pizza and potato chips are left over if you had the teenagers Sunday school party at your house. *(If there is any pizza left over, there's something wrong with your teenagers, by the way.)*

Exercises for Sunday School Teachers:

If you teach toddlers — *lift weights to strengthen arms and back for picking up your charges.*

If you teach children — *Do 20 knee-bends daily to stay in shape for getting in and out of those little chairs.*

If you teach teenagers — *take dancing lessons. Otherwise you'll feel like Methuselah when you chaperone their class parties.*

If you teach young adults — *jog two miles daily so the yuppies will identify with you.*

If you teach older adults — *get a rocking chair and practice rocking.*

The Sex Life of Sunday School Teachers:

Studies by five New York sex therapists indicate that married Sunday school teachers have successful and satisfying sex lives — except on Sunday mornings when they are all frantically studying the Sunday school lesson.

Single Sunday school teachers are always celibate. That's what the survey said.

SUNDAY SCHOOL
TEACHER'S PRAYER

Dear Lord, as I begin to teach
Another class today,
I pray for guidance from above
To say what I should say.
May all my words and attitudes
Reflect your love and care.
May I a good example be:
Help me my faith to share.
I pray to live as I should live,
And in your pathways walk.
And one more thing, if you don't mind,
Please help me find the chalk.

Dress for Success in Sunday School:

If you teach preschoolers, wear something disposable or plastic.

If you teach children, wear an apron with a Care Bear™ on the pocket.

If you teach middle-school kids, wear a spitball-proof vest.

If you teach high-school kids, dress right out of *Seventeen* or *G.Q.*

If you teach the college crowd, wear something from *L. L. Bean*.

If you teach the little old ladies, carry a clean handkerchief.

If you teach the men's class, wear anything that's about three years out of style.

IF YOU TEACH MIDDLE SCHOOL KIDS...

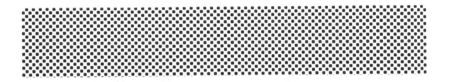

Sources Of Help For Sunday School Teachers:

Sunday school teachers who need counseling on matters theological, spiritual or educational are advised to consult the following experts in these areas:

Pope John Paul II
Billy Graham
Mother Theresa
The Archbishop of Canterbury
Norman Vincent Peale
Sunday School Sue

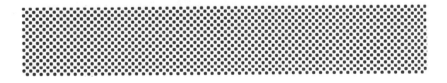

Chapter 5:
SO YOU'RE NO STEPHEN SPIELBERG?
Getting the Attention of Youth

ROBERT READFORD

N o one can accuse Robert Readford of not using the recommended curriculum materials. Every Sunday he reads the lesson in the quarterly to his class — word for word.

There are a number of reasons Robert reads to his class. To start with, they are teenagers, and Robert is afraid they know more than he does. After all, he didn't graduate from college, and he doesn't own or operate a computer. Like the vast majority of Sunday school teachers, Robert doesn't consider himself particularly clever or creative. His job keeps him pretty

ONE EYE FOR KEEPING ON THE CLOCK

EAR MUFFS TO MUFFLE CLASS QUESTIONS

LESSON MATERIAL TO READ WITHOUT LOOKING UP

CROSSED FINGERS JUST IN CASE SOMEONE ASKS A STICKY QUESTION

EXTRA READING MATERIAL TO FILL ENTIRE CLASS TIME

ROBERT READFORD

busy, and he doesn't have a lot of time to spend studying the lesson or coming up with new and different activities for his class. So he reads to them.

Robert is smart enough to realize that curriculum writers are well versed in Biblical and theological matters, so he depends entirely on their expertise, not departing one comma's worth from their words.

Fielding a question from a class member strikes terror in Robert's heart, so he wimps out and doesn't allow time for discussion. If he thinks there's a possibililty that reading the lesson won't use up the class time, he brings something else to read, so there will not be a second left in which anyone could ask some sticky question like where Cain and Abel got their wives.

Sometimes Robert does encourage class participation by having students read aloud from the Sunday school book. He probably does more to promote silent prayer than any other teacher in the church. Throughout the class session, poor readers slink down in their chairs and pray fervently that they will not be called on to read. Good readers pray to be delivered from enduring any more of the poor readers' stammering and stumbling. Meanwhile, Robert is praying that no one will ask him about Cain and Abel's wives.

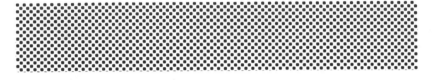

Names To Drop Around Teenagers:

1. John Cougar Mellencamp
2. Billy Joel
3. Bruce Springsteen
4. Dale Murphy
5. Sheila E.
6. Madonna
7. Herschel Walker
8. Van Halen
9. Prince
10. Tina Turner

Names Teenagers Won't Know:

1. Perry Como
2. Bing Crosby
3. The Kingston Trio
4. Spiro Agnew
5. Margaret O'Brien
6. Esther Williams
7. Mario Lanza
8. J. Edgar Hoover
9. Peter, Paul and Mary
10. Cass Elliot

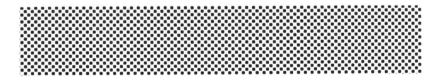

TEENAGERS AND SUNDAY SCHOOL

If you think Madonna is the Virgin Mary, "The Boss" is your superior at work, and Alabama is just a southern state, you are probably not a teenager or a teacher of teenagers.

If you teach teenagers in Sunday school, you might have been tempted at times to tap dance naked on the piano to get their attention. After all, how's a Sunday school teacher to compete with spectacular culture videos, movies, TV, theme parks, and the Trans Ams and Corvettes waiting in the church parking lot? Even the schools don't make it any easier. The computers and other sophisticated teaching equipment in public school classrooms can make the simple format of Sunday school seem pretty dull. What's a teacher to do?

How do you appeal to and communicate with a teenager? What's the secret combination that unlocks the magic door and allows teacher and student to relate as two human beings?

Maybe the starting point is the realization that all teenagers are not alike. Teens recognize and define several distinct subcultures within their own world. Each group has its own dress code, customs and rules of behavior. These groups are found in most high schools and are identified by such names as jocks, preppies, leather jacket crowd, socialites, druggies, straights, norms, punks, breakers and nerds.

During this conformist stage of life, kids depend on the expectation of others as the norm. Their self-identity is determined by the group to which they belong. It might appear that members of each group are attempting to be clones of the leader, but in reality, they want to be part of their group and still be acknowledged as the individuals they are.

Differences such as race, physical and mental abilities, socio-economic background, and religious upbringing make it obvious that there is no such thing as a typical teenager.

However, there are a number of things that many teens do have in common. Those who don't have a car want one as desperately as a drowning man wants air. Those who have a car want a newer, sportier model. Most high-school students who are gainfully employed quickly convert paychecks into car payments.

Also, most current high-school students are well on their way to permanent hearing impairment. Sunday school teachers may find it necessary to speak extra loudly to kids accustomed to rock music that measures five on the Richter scale. For those

85

SIGN LANGUAGE MAY SOMETIMES BE ADVISABLE

with earphones permanently attached, sign language might work.

Normal but nevertheless amazing growth spurts, accompanied by enormous appetites and lots of glandular activity quickly turn awkward, figity, noisy kids into individuals who walk around in adult bodies while still operating with the knowledge, understanding, judgment and emotions of a teenager.

Because of rapid emotional and physical changes, teens are frequently moody. As they mature intellectually and socially, many have a know-it-all attitude and a propensity for going to extremes that cause their parents and teachers to think seriously about putting them in a cage. All this is part of their growing need for independence and should be endured heroically.

86

People in their teen years appear to be self-centered because they are trying to determine what is uniquely their own terms of standards and beliefs. Their Sunday school teachers will be rewarded with a crown, white robe and special self-cleaning harp for sticking by them as they wade through the sometimes difficult process of giving shape and substance to their own faith.

Fortunately, teenagers don't bite Sunday school teachers. The vast majority are good kids who respond favorably to efforts by adults to guide and instruct them, and as a rule, they're a barrel of fun to be around.

Special Problems of Today's Youth

High on any teenager's problem list are relationships with peers, relationships with parents, and relationships between the sexes. Most of them spend a great deal of time thinking about how they look, how well others like them, and whether or not they have anything interesting lined up for the weekend.

Usually they are concerned about school work, popularity, friendship, cars, music, social activities, sports, love, sex, dating, marriage, money, acne and measurements of bust, waist and hips.

Frequently teenagers are not as happy-go-lucky as they appear. Many worry a lot. They are curious, which leads to experimentation with alcohol, drugs and sex, but they are also highly sensitive to religious inclinations and moral dilemmas.

Moral issues for today's youth are more complex than they were for their parents. Decisions now must be made on tougher problems than whether or not to attend Sunday ballgames and movies. The sexual revolution has called into question not only sexual mores, but roles as well. Cocaine, college costs, nuclear holocaust, interracial dating, terrorist attacks, the rising rate in teenage suicides, S.A.T. scores, and Aids all give teenagers plenty to think about.

Youth are vulnerable because they want to be loved and to belong. They are highly idealistic and want to change the world, so they are prime targets for cults which can destroy them psychologically and spiritually.

Girls think they should look like fashion models, so they fall into eating disorders like anorexia nervosa and bulimia.

Because family patterns have changed drastically, about

87

three out of ten kids under eighteen don't live in typical two-parent families. One in ten live with one parent and a step-parent, and two in ten live with just one parent. For these young people, the problems of growing up are intensified. Many face financial strains, feelings of being different, residential instability, loss of security, the lack of a role model, and countless other adjustments that arise when parents divorce and go through the dating and re-marriage process.

Sunday school teachers might not set out to be role models and security figures for the kids in their classes, but many of them are, whether they planned it that way or not.

Needs of Youth That Sunday School Teachers Can Help Fill

Although Sunday school teachers can't give their class members cars and be their absent parents, they can help fill some very specific needs.

Frequently teenagers have difficulty talking to their parents — even when the teenagers are good kids and the parents would love to be number one confidant and advisor. Sunday school teachers who can meet students on their own levels, and who can be a friend, not a judge, might be the adult that teenagers choose to talk with about their problems.

Youth need self-understanding and acceptance as well as understanding and acceptance from adults. They need to do for themselves and work toward independence from their families. They need freedom to be themselves, to cooperate or to rebel, to agree or to disagree, to express an opinion or not, to belong, but not be held captive. At the same time they need guidance and direction from adults, and a feeling of security and stability in an insecure and unstable world. They need adult examples of behavior and thinking characteristic of Christians. They need a Christian faith to steady them and assure them that they are forgiven, accepted and born again. Sunday school teachers who are secure in their own beliefs, but not dogmatic and judgmental, can help fill these needs of teenagers.

ROBERT READFORD: EVEN YOU CAN BECOME THE IDEAL SUNDAY SCHOOL TEACHER

The ideal teacher of teenagers would have the enthusiasm and energy of Mary Lou Retton, the creative genius of Steven Spielberg, the concern and Christian commitment of Mother Teresa, the educational expertise of John Dewey, the Biblical knowledge of William Barclay, the sense of humor of Phyllis Diller, and the prayer life of the Pope.

Of course there is no such animal. Like Robert Readford, most Sunday school teachers have glaring shortcomings, but they teach anyway for a variety of reasons. What could Robert Readford do to improve his teaching? How could he gain the courage and self-confidence to try new teaching methods? How could he establish a meaningful relationship with the teenagers in his class?

One of the most helpful things Robert could do would be to get to know his students — "where they're coming from." He could encourage them to talk about their concerns, and to try and be a friend to them. He could do this not only at Sunday school, but by attending some of their ballgames, plays and other functions that are important to the teenagers.

Robert needs to realize that he is teaching people, not just a lesson. His goal with the lesson should be not to cover it, but to uncover it so students can discover its truth for themselves.

He could begin by giving careful attention to the suggestions in the teacher's guide. To use the suggestions he finds there, he will have to plan ahead, and it won't be nearly as easy as reading aloud to the class.

Robert could have a student planning committee to study the lesson ahead of time and make suggestions to him about which parts they consider most interesting, and what they would like to discuss on Sunday mornings. They could suggest activities and approaches that they would like him to use in class.

Robert could also make assignments to students. These should be simple at first, like finding the answer to one question and reporting on it in class. It's important that Robert assign questions that students can find answers to. He should be prepared to tell them where to look for the answers. Through the telephone conversations necessary to handle the assignments, Robert can begin to get to know his students better.

A teacher like Robert who needs increased confidence in his teaching could benefit from team teaching. This is not alternating Sundays or months or quarters. In team teaching, both teachers are there every Sunday. They plan the lesson together and share teaching responsibilities during class time. Team teachers can learn from and support one another, and the team approach will add variety and interest.

There is no need for Robert Readford or any other teacher to try and measure up to some phony ideal of the perfect teacher who has all the answers and has reached glorified sanctification. As Robert gets to know his class members, they will get to know him, and they can experience the freedom of being themselves. Robert can find the freedom to say, "I don't know." He can be engaged with his students in a shared search for truth.

What Teenagers Want In A Sunday School Teacher

Teenagers want teachers who are not boring, not condescending, not preachy and not judgmental. They want teachers who are open, honest and willing to listen and discuss. They want teachers who have a faith to share and who recognize the talents, abilities and uncertainties of youth.

The effective teacher of teenagers is patient, tolerant and understanding. He or she gives guidance and support without holding the reins too tightly and without relinquishing leadership completely.

A good teacher guides students and leaves room for them to debate and discover things for themselves. He or she encourages and enables learners to think, seek, ponder, try, and

THE EFFECTIVE TEACHER IS PATIENT, TOLERANT, UNDERSTANDING

grow. The good teacher knows that when learners figure it out for themselves, they internalize what they have learned, and it is really theirs.

Teenagers probably learn a lot more from the lifestyle of their teacher than from their words.

Getting Youth Involved In A Meaningful Discussion

Teenagers don't always know what they think about a

given topic, and usually, even if they think they know what they think, they can't verbalize it effectively. A properly handled discussion gives them the opportunity to think through questions, and it provides valuable practice in self-expression.

The first rule for leading a discussion among youth is to be sure you have something to discuss. Have a discussion on something specific like a film the kids have seen, a study they have made, a lecture they have heard, or a particular experience they have had.

Here are some tips for leading a meaningful discussion:

1. *Choose a topic that is of real concern to the teenagers.*
2. *Get as many involved as possible.*
3. *Start with easy questions. Work up to "leading" questions.*
4. *Keep it informal and friendly (no heated arguments).*
5. *Don't "put down" anybody's contribution.*
6. *Encourage short contributions rather than long speeches.*
7. *Keep the discussion on track. (Listing on the chalkboard questions to be covered helps do this.)*
8. *Encourage concrete examples rather than abstract ideas when possible.*
9. *Remain open-minded.*
10. *Summarize findings, agreements, disagreements, conclusions and questions for further study.*

A Word About Older Youth and Younger Youth

In small churches, 13-year-olds may sometimes find themselves in a class with 18-year-olds. If there is any way to avoid this, by all means, avoid this!

There is a world of difference in the middle school child and the high-school senior. It's almost impossible to have a meaningful discussion or lesson for one age group without being above or below the attention span, interest level, comprehension and concerns of the other age group.

Younger teens needs lots of activity to channel and

control all that energy, nervousness, punching, elbowing and kicking that seventh and eighth graders are so full of. They need workbooks, games and stories that are inappropriate for older youth.

College age youth have more excuses for not attending Sunday school than Imelda Marcos has shoes. They will work to save the whales, save the pandas, save the snail darter and save the environment, but if you count on them, you'll never save the Sunday school.

Don't combine classes of older teenagers with younger ones. A two or three year age span is more than enough for teenage groups.

How Can Youth Feel More A Part Of The Church?

Often times adults become frustrated with teenagers because teenagers don't seem to take their church responsibilities seriously enough. A fairly typical attitude among some adult church members is, "Those kids just want to be entertained and fed. When are they going to learn to contribute a little something to the life of the church themselves?" Teenagers' apparent lack of responsibility may be a response to adults who haven't let the youth make decisions and commitments.

The teacher of teenagers must guide students along and show them how to do whatever they're supposed to do. It's easier for the teacher or parents to do it than to stay behind the kids and show them exactly how to do it. But that's not the way to teach responsibility.

Here are some ways teenagers can contribute to the life of the congregation:

1. *Singing in the choir*
2. *Ushering*
3. *Assisting in the nursery (Be careful here, or they'll never attend the worship service.)*
4. *Serving as acolytes*
5. *Visiting shut-ins and nursing home residents*
6. *Providing fellowship events such as skit nights, talent shows, etc.*
7. *Leading in Sunday night or mid-week services*

8. *Contributing financially from their allowances or jobs*

9. *Helping with recreation at Vacation Bible School*

10. *Getting involved with church-wide service projects*

TEENS CAN CONTRIBUTE IN SEVERAL WAYS

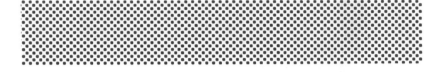

Questions Of Deep And Abiding Concern To Sunday School Teachers:

1. Am I meeting the needs of my students?
2. Am I boring my students?
3. Do my students understand what I am trying to teach?
4. Do my students care about what I am trying to teach?
5. Where's the chalk?

Guaranteed Attention-Getters For A Lethargic Class:

1. Tell them there's a hidden treasure, and the clues will be revealed in the lesson.
2. Record the lesson on tape and tell them it's a demonic message being played backward.
3. Tell them there will be an exam at the end of the lesson, and the results will go down on their permanent records.
4. Tell them someone threatened your life if you teach this lesson, but you're going to teach it anyway.
5. Tap dance naked on the piano.

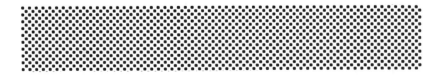

Sunday School Sue

Dear Sunday School Sue,

I teach a class of eighth graders. I'm won-dering if a contagious bladder disease is run-ning rampant through our class. Either some of them have serious physical problems, or they are having a party in the boys' restroom during Sun-day school.

About five minutes into the lesson the boys start asking permission to go to the restroom. I'm afraid not to let them go. I mean, after all, who knows about that sort of thing? If one stays in the men's room an unusually long time and I send another to check on him, neither returns. Some Sundays we have as many as five or six out of the class at one time because they "just have to go."

I'm no dummy. I think they are hiding in there to get out of Sunday school. What do you think? My problem is, I'm a woman, and I hesi-tate to go into the men's room to see what's going on. What do you suggest?

Curious in Carson City

Dear Curious,

I'm no dummy either, and I think you've about got it figured out. I would suggest that you station a father of one of the boys in the men's room on Sunday morn-ing to escort the boys back to class as soon as feasible. If you don't want to do that, just wait until over fifty percent of the class is in the restroom, and then move the remain-ing students in there for Sunday school. It might not be the best place in the world for teaching, but it will free up a room that is probably needed for a newly organized class.

Sunday School Sue

Chapter 6:
THE B-I-B-L-E
That's the Book for Me

PERCY PROOF-TEXT

Percy Proof-Text can quote Bible verses that he believes prove exactly when the world was created and the precise moment it will come to an end. He can cite chapter and verse that tell the exact number of Jews who will be in Heaven, where the ark is now located, and why you shouldn't take blood transfusions.

According to Percy, there are scripture quotations that refer to the Nazis in World War II Germany, the expulsion of the Shah of Iran, and the Star Wars space program. He's able

CLASS SCOREBOARD

THE WORD

OTHER WORDS

PERCY PROOF-TEXT

to point out references to the number of helicopters in the Israeli Air Force, and he can tell you the role these machines will play in the Rapture. He manages to do this by using verses to prove points they were never intended to apply to, but you can't convince him of that.

Percy Proof-Text delights in finding passages that he believes are prophesies soon to be fulfilled. He'll share with you information from the Bible about Colonel Moammar Khadafy, the Rev. Louis Farrakhan, and the European Common Market. Of course Percy admits that the Bible doesn't call them by those names, but he doesn't worry about that.

If the Bible says the earth is flat and four-cornered, then Percy believes the earth is flat and four-cornered. He sees the Bible as the world's single source of truth on all matters. For answers to questions on science, geography, economics and medicine, Percy Proof-Text always turns to the Bible. Seeing the Bible as infallible, Percy believes it is scientifically accurate. He doesn't believe man really ever walked on the moon, because he can't find a reference to it in the scriptures. He's not sure, but he thinks all those television pictures of the moon walk were really made in Arizona.

Percy Proof-Text has an all-or-nothing-at-all approach to the Bible. He believes that every jot and tittle is of equal value and inspiration, and if you can't accept all of it as inherent, then none of it has merit.

The King James Version is Percy's favorite. Percy does not believe that writers of the Bible were limited by their historical circumstances. He imagines that the Lord magically transmitted it, word for word, to the writers, and by something like automatic writing, they penned the numbered verses, which have been miraculously preserved, with the words of Christ in red ink.

Unfortunately, Percy teaches a class of high-school students who have also come to believe in the all-or-nothing-at-all approach. The problem is, some are so turned off by Percy's narrow-mindedness, that they decided to believe nothing-at-all of the Bible.

DIBS AND DABS BIBLE STORIES

Once upon a time there was a man who had two sons; and the younger of them said to him, "Father, give me the share of property that falls to me." So he gathered all he had and took his journey into a far country.

And as he was going down from Jerusalem to Jericho, he fell among robbers who stripped him, beat him and cast him into a pit in the wilderness. Now the daughter of Pharoah came down and saw the boy, and lo he was crying, and she sent her maid to fetch him out of the pit. And Pharoah's daughter took him to the palace, and he became her son.

And being exhausted, he fell asleep on the palace roof, and as he slept, he had a dream. He saw something descending like a great sheet, and in it were all kinds of animals and reptiles and birds of the air. And the Lord told him to take two of every living thing that he saw and put them into an ark of gopher wood, along with all his household.

And he took the ark out onto the lake, and behold there was a great wind and a mighty tempest, so that the ship threatened to break up. And the Lord appointed a great fish to swallow the ship. And after forty days and forty nights, the fish spit the ship onto dry land where a great famine arose, and among all the people there were only five barley loaves and two fishes to eat. The trees no longer bore good fruit, so he cursed the fig trees and called down tongues of fire on the olive trees.

And when he came to himself, he determined to return to the palace. But as he was traveling, behold a great light blinded him, and all the animals, two by two, were turned into a pillar of salt. But an angel of the Lord appeared unto him, and the glory of the Lord shown round about him, and a voice said unto him, "Put off your shoes from your feet, for the place on which you are standing is holy ground. Go unto the land that I will show you, and cast not your pearls before swine." And so he went into a strange country where he met a shepherd who said, "I must go and bury

HOLY GROUND PLEASE REMOVE YOUR RUBBERS

my father; feed my sheep." But the boy lost 99 of the sheep, and when the shepherd returned, he said unto the boy, "You wicked and slothful servant." And the shepherd shaved off seven locks of the boy's head, and his strength left him.

And a mighty giant picked him up and cast him into a den of lions, but the boy took five smooth stones from his pocket, turned the stones into bread, and fed it to the lions. Now I ask you, is it more blessed to give than to receive?

(When Bible study is no more than dibs and dabs of stories told out of context, this is what you get.)

THE BIBLE AND SUNDAY SCHOOL

Some folks fall into Percy Proof-Text's bear trap of misusing scripture. Some slide down the slippery slope to meaninglessness by taking the dibs and dabs approach to Bible stories, with no concept of the one story the Bible tells. There are those who see the Bible only as a rule book for living, and those who think it is no more than a collection of lofty ethical principles. For some, the Bible is the source of authoritative doctrines, and for others it is a collection of inspirational materials to be used in group and private devotions. And then there are those for whom the Bible is merely a venerated object that is dusted carefully as it resides in its place of honor on the coffee table.

Even for Sunday school teachers, the Bible is often mysterious and difficult to understand. Perhaps that's because many of us don't really know what the Bible is, how it came to be, and how we should go about studying it.

What Is The Bible And Where Did It Come From?

We have all been taught that the Bible is God's Word, Holy Scripture, inspired sacred literature. And so it is. But it is also helpful to know that the Bible is a collection of books. The word BIBLE comes from the Greek "biblia," meaning "books." The Bible is a compilation of ancient writings about God and his relationship to the Hebrew people and later the Christian church.

To understand the Bible and to teach its truths effectively to others, Sunday school teachers need to be aware that there are many types of writings in the Bible. The Bible contains letters, poetry, law, songs, histories, wise sayings, short stories and orations, just to name a few. When you read a passage of scripture, you need to know what kind of writing it is. There are some pretty distinct differences between religious poetry and history. Being able to distinguish one from the other helps in understanding a Bible passage.

Contrary to a common misconception, God did not hand the Bible down from the sky one day. It took approximately a thousand years — about 900 B.C. to about 100 A.D. — for the Bible to be written. Countless people were involved in the process — copyists and editors as well as writers. The Bible was written in a number of places. Parts of it originated in Palestine, some in Babylon, Egypt, Rome, Corinth and other locations.

The Old Testament was originally written in Hebrew, and the New Testament was originally written in Greek. There are no copies of any original manuscripts in existence. When we read the Bible, we read a translation of a copy.

The Bible is a very diverse book, but it has a unity because of the one story it tells. The Bible tells the story of man's encounter with God in the crucial events of history. These stories are about the *Old Agreement* between God and the Hebrews, and the great themes of their faith: the promise of the patriarchs, the divine deliverance from Egypt, the guidance in the wilderness wanderings, the giving of the law at Sinai, and the inheritance of the promised land. It relates accounts of Israel's history as seen through the eyes of men of God.

The New Testament tells the story of the *New Agreement* between God and man based on the life and teachings of Jesus Christ. It includes a history of the early Christian church as it became the vehicle for spreading the news that *all* people could have a relationship with God.

Over the years, the scriptures became widely accepted as authoritative because of their meaning for and inspiration to the people of God. The writings were acknowledged as sacred (canonized) by official councils of the early church.

Taking The Bible Seriously

If you are going to take the Bible seriously, you must always take it in context, asking not only what it says, but what it means. Several questions should be asked about any passage of scripture. Newspaper reporters always cover the *who, what, when, where* and *why* of a topic. That's a good idea for students of the Bible as well.

With a little help from a commentary or Bible dictionary, you can seek answers, answers that will usually raise more

STUDY THE BIBLE AS IF YOU ARE A NEWS REPORTER

questions. But seek them anyway. You'll be glad you did. Sometimes you might learn that even the most erudite Bible scholars don't know the answers to your questions, but you can bet your bottom dollar, they've dealt with the questions up one side and down the other.

Ask *who* wrote a passage and to *whom* it was written. *What* kind of literature is it? *What* is the whole passage about, not just one or two verses of it? *When* was the passage written? That often gives a clue to its original meaning and authorship. Knowing *where* it was written can help you know more about its original purpose and meaning. *Why* was the passage written? What was it originally intended to convey? *Why* did the early church find enough meaning and significance in it to acknowledge it as sacred scripture?

If we know the original purpose of a verse or chapter in the Bible, we can get a clearer understanding of its meaning for us today. And of course the whole purpose of studying the Bible is to know what it has to say to us and our lives. Just as God inspired people to write the Bible, he inspires people as they read the Bible. A careful, prayerful consideration of scripture passages, taken in context helps us know God and grow in faith and discipleship.

Some Tips To Remember

All parts of the Bible do not have equal meaning and value for us. If you don't believe that, read Numbers 15:2-10, and see if that inspires you as much as John 3:16, or Matthew 22:37-40.

The whole Bible must be understood in the light of the life and teachings of Jesus Christ. When we read Old Testament accounts of the atrocities committed in the name of God, we are horrified and bewildered. How could such things be in the Bible? Remember that writers of the Old Testament had an incomplete idea about God. Early concepts of God and his nature gradually gave way to an understanding of the nature of God as seen in Christ. Too often we think there was one God for the Old Testament and another for the New Testament. That's not true, of course. God does not change, but man's understanding of God changes. God has always been loving, just, righteous, merciful and forgiving, but people have not always realized that.

The writers of the Bible were products of the historical circumstances in which they lived. Old Testament writers did not have the benefit of having known Jesus. Those men of God who wrote about God's revelation of himself and people's response to that revelation were limited by the scientific and philosophical viewpoints of their day. So anytime we read a verse of scripture, we must let the Bible speak on its own terms.

Being a Bible student does not mean refusing to think. God gave us minds to study and reason. Our purpose is not to worship a book. That would be Bibliolotry. We worship God, and we learn of him through a book. Our faith rests on our relationship with Christ, and when that is solid and secure, we are free to deal honestly with the deep and complicated questions presented to us in the Bible.

Bible study is not an end in itself. It is a means of our becoming what God would have us become.

Some Types Of Literature In The Bible:

(If you can find out which type you're dealing with, you'll find it a lot easier to understand.)

History
Poetry
Hymns
Legal Codes
Prophecies
Wise Sayings
Letters
Orations
Reflective Literature
Missionary Tracts
Sermons
Short Stories
Liturgical Direc-
tions
Census of People
Philosophy
Visions
Gospels
Love Lyrics
Official Records
Personal Memoirs

"WOW! GET A LOAD OF THESE LYRICS!"

THERE ARE MANY TYPES OF LITERATURE IN THE BIBLE

People Who Have All The Answers To Your Biblical Questions:

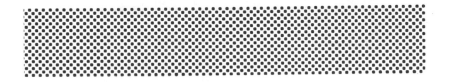

Common Uses For The Bible:

1. Excellent for pressing that rosebud you want to keep.
2. Even better for pressing four-leaf clovers.
3. Looks good on coffee table.
4. Safe place to hide secret papers.
5. Also good for hiding money.
6. If left in a conspicuous spot on your desk, it will impress clients with your holiness.
7. Good location for record of your family tree.
8. Carry it to church. It's a nice compliment to your Sunday suit.
9. If placed on the dashboard of your car, it might influence the patrolman not to give you a ticket for speeding.
10. Can be read and studied to increase religious knowledge, strengthen faith and broaden understanding of yourself, others and God. Also helpful guide for Christian living.

Sunday School Sue

Dear Sunday School Sue,

I joined a weekday Bible study group because I want to study the Bible. Well, if that's Bible study, I'm the queen of Peru.

Very little time is spent reading or discussing the Bible. Ususally someone reads a verse or two of scripture and tells how much it means to her. Nearly all of the hour is devoted to prayer requests. Whenever prayer is requested for anyone, we all have to hear every detail of whatever the problem is that we should pray about. Very often it's a juicy tale about someone's marital difficulties or job problems. These concerns are not limited to group members or even church members. Anyone in town whose spouse is having an affair, who got the ax at the office, or whose kids are messing with pot is discussed and prayed about.

To tell the truth, I'm not learning a thing about the Bible, but I know every tidbit of news about anyone within a 20-mile radius.

Are all Bible study groups like this? Is there another way I can get involved in group Bible study?

Disappointed in Detroit

Dear Disappointed,

The answers to your questions, in order, are no and yes. Talk to your minister and ask him to recommend an adult Sunday school class in your church that is involved in Bible study. If there is not a class in existence that appeals to you, volunteer to help organize one. See if the minister or some other capable Bible student will get things rolling with a short-term study on a book of the Bible that especially interests

you. Be sure the group uses Bible study curriculum materials approved by your denomination. Also be sure to invite members of the weekday Bible study group to attend your new Sunday school class. Once they see what a real Bible study is like, they will probably want to change their format. It's very likely that others in the weekday group share your feelings and would also like to study something more than the personal difficulties of others.

Meanwhile, send a prayer request to the weekday group. Ask them to pray for all the gossips in town.

Sunday School Sue

Dear Sunday School Sue,

Please don't think I'm the world's biggest dummy, but I'm relatively new at teaching Sunday school, and what I don't know is almost everything. I hear other teachers speaking of how helpful commentaries and concordances are to them as they prepare their lessons. I'm embarrassed to admit that I have never used a commentary, and I have not the foggiest idea what a concordance is. What are they, where could I find them, and what do I do with them once I get them?

Embarrassed in Evanston

Dear Embarrassed,

Don't be. Studies show that everyone is ignorant about something. Studies also show that many Sunday school teachers have never been exposed to commentaries and concordances. There's also another reference work that Sunday school teachers need to use — the Bible dictionary. Here's some information about all three.

A BIBLE DICTIONARY is a reference book that lists alphabetically, significant terms and names found in the Bible. Most Bible dictionaries give a great deal of helpful information about people, places and

events in the Bible. Some include definitions and explanations of major theological concepts and biblical doctrines, as well as articles on history, archeology and geography. Many have cross references, maps, illustrations and pronunciation guides. Any time you come upon a word in the Bible you don't understand, look it up. For instance, in reading the parable of the talents, look up the word TALENT, and you'll learn that is has nothing to do with playing the accordian or doing a soft-shoe routine.

A BIBLE COMMENTARY is a volume or set of volumes that includes a systematic series of explanations and interpretations of Bible passages by chapter and verse. They usually include summaries of each book of the Bible, and introductory information about authorship, date and background of the text. Many include indexes, maps and general articles that shed light on Bible passages. Commentaries are life

THERE ARE BIBLE STUDY AIDS IN YOUR
CHURCH AND PUBLIC LIBRARIES

savers when it comes to comprehending meanings in difficult to understand passages. Frequently commentaries not only clarify the meaning of the text, but apply it to people's daily needs and concerns.

A CONCORDANCE is an alphabetical index of the principle words in Bible verses. For example, say you wanted to find the verse that says, "My soul doth magnify the Lord," but you have no idea where to begin looking for it. Decide what the key word is in the verse, and look it up., In this case, you could look up SOUL or MAGNIFY. All passages in the Bible that contain those words will be listed in order in the concordance, within the phrase in which they occur, along with the chapter and verse. A little practice with a concordance and you will be locating Bible passages very quickly. Concordances are also great for topical studies. In other words, if you are teaching a lesson on jealousy, and you want to know more than your lesson book tells about the subject, just look up the word JEALOUS, and the concordance will direct you to every verse in the Bible that deals with the subject.

HELPFUL BIBLE STUDY
REFERENCE BOOKS

THE NEW HARPER'S BIBLE DICTIONARY, by Madeleine S, and J. Lane Miller (Harper)

THE WESTMINSTER CONCISE BIBLE DICTIONARY, by Barbara Smith (Westminster)

THE NEW WESTMINSTER DICTIONARY OF THE BIBLE, edited by Henry Snyder Gehman (Westminster)

THE INTERPRETER'S ONE-VOLUME COMMENTARY ON THE BIBLE, edited by Charles M. Laymon (Abingdon)

THE ABINGDON BIBLE COMMENTARY, edited by Frederick Carl Eiselen,

Edwin Lewis, and David G. Downey (Doubleday)

THE INTERPRETER'S CONCISE COMMENTARY (Abingdon)

THE LAYMAN'S BIBLE COMMEN-TARY (John Knox)

THE WESTMINSTER HISTORICAL ATLAS TO THE BIBLE, edited by G. Ernest Wright and Floyd V. Filson (Westminster)

THE BIBLE COMPANION (Abington)

CRUDEN'S COMPLETE CONCOR-DANCE (Zondervan)

ABINGDON'S STRONG'S EXHAUS-TIVE CONCORDANCE OF THE BIBLE, James Strong (Abingdon)

THE DICTIONARY OF THE BIBLE AND RELIGION, William H. Gentz, Gen-eral Editor (Abingdon)

THE INTERPRETER'S BIBLE (Ab-ingdon)

This is by no means an exhaustive list of Bible study helps. There are many com-mentaries, atlases, Bible dictionaries and concordances on the market. Prices of the above reference books range from $5.99 for a paperback edition of a Bible dictionary to $255 for a super deluxe twelve volume set of commentaries. Many of them are proba-bly in your church or public library. All can be ordered from:

> *Cokesbury Service Center*
> *1635 Adrian Road*
> *Burlingame, CA 94010*
>
> *or*
>
> *Cokesbury Service Center*
> *201 Eighth Avenue, South*
> *P.O. Box 801*
> *Nashville, TN 37202*

Before you invest in expensive refer-ence books, talk to your minister and ask him to let you look at some of his books. He will probably be happy to recommend what he has found helpful. Also, try to visit a

112

bookstore that specializes in this kind of thing and spend some time browsing. It's great fun. And don't ever be too embarrassed to ask.

Sunday School Sue

HOW JESUS USED THE BIBLE

The Master Teacher used the Bible as one of his main teaching resources. The only Bible he had was the Old Testament, but he knew it well, and he quoted from it extensively.

Jesus did not use legalistic interpretations of scripture to make his points. He was more interested in obedience to the spirit of the word rather than the letter of the law.

Because Jesus believed that God continues to reveal himself, he heeded not only the words of scripture, but the voice of God within him as well.

Jesus made the scriptures relevant to people's daily lives. He used examples from day-to-day experiences with which people could identify. He took generalities from the Old Testament and applied them to specific concerns of the people he taught.

Accounts of the temptation in the wilderness and the crucifixion are examples of Jesus' turning to the Bible for strength and help in times of his deepest personal agonies.

If he had had access to Bible dictionaries, commentaries and concordances, he probably would have used those too.

USING THE BIBLE WITH CHILDREN

You know you have a problem when you realize that many people think Sunday school is just for children, and yet the Bible is a book written for adults.

Obviously no one suggests waiting until people become adults to begin teaching the Bible to them. At the same time, no one with good sense would suggest teaching the Bible to children in the same way it is taught to adults. Effective teaching will always take into account the nature of the Bible and the nature of children. Children learn the message of the Bible through relationships with adults who believe in and affirm the Bible.

Toddlers

Even toddlers can be aware that the Bible is a special book about God and Jesus. They can know that the Bible in the Sunday school room is the same book as the Bible at home. They can comprehend some simply told stories from the Bible that relate to their experiences. Repetition is important with very young children. They benefit from hearing very brief versions of stories and verses repeated over and over. They can also sing songs based on Bible verses appropriate for them.

It's not too difficult to figure out that many stories in the Bible are inappropriate for very young children. Subjects that would frighten or confuse or seem to emphasize the magical should be avoided. Stories that shed light on a child's daily experiences will be more meaningful. Positive stories of Jesus and God and their care and love are always fitting selections.

At this age, children learn more from experiencing the message of the Bible being lived out in the lives of their teachers and parents than from hearing the words of the Bible.

Kindergarten

Four, five, and six-year-olds can deal with the Bible in all the ways the toddler can, plus some. They can sit still longer and listen to a story for several minutes, so the stories need not be as abbreviated as those told to toddlers. It is important that they be allowed to handle the Bible. Children who have not yet learned to read will probably enjoy pretending to read from the Bible. They should be encouraged to study and talk about pictures that show Bible stories and unfamiliar Bible customs. They can participate in simple dramatizations of Bible stories. All stories told or sung should be related to children's experiences.

Children learn more about the love of God through their relationships to adults who love God than through hearing words about it.

Elementary Children

Younger children can only comprehend the here and now, but as they get into the elementary years, they begin to be aware that things happened a long time ago. They will understand that the Bible is very old, and that it is God's special book, or it would not have survived throughout the centuries. Children who can read some of the Bible for themselves will

LET CHILDREN PARTICIPATE IN SIMPLE BIBLE DRAMATIZATIONS

enjoy having their own personal copy of the Bible and learning to look up passages for themselves. Many will be especially interested in how people lived in Bible times. Elementary children will enjoy learning about the Bible through stories and riddles. They can dramatize and illustrate Bible stories.

Older elementary children will enjoy discussing the meaning of passages. They can understand that God speaks in people's minds when they read the Bible. Fifth and sixth graders can study about how the Bible came to be, and they will understand that the Bible contains many different types of literature. They can make time lines to locate biblical events in history, and they will probably want to paraphrase scripture passages or write modern versions of a Bible story.

God reveals himself to us in many ways, one of which is the Bible. As children learn the message of the Bible and comprehend its meaning, they build a basic foundation for a faith that can grow and allow for a commitment to Christ and a Christian lifestyle.

Chapter 7:
BLESS THE BEASTS
OR CHILDREN

SARA SURROGATE

Sara Surrogate started teaching the third and fourth graders about a year ago, but the kids in the class still are not sure what she looks like. Sara is at Sunday school so seldom that the greeters at the door usually try to give her a visitor's ribbon.

There are many reasons for Sara's imperfect attendance. Some Sundays her in-laws visit, and she has to stay home and cook. There are times when her husband has a business trip that includes the weekend, and she accompanies him. Sometimes it's an out-of-town ballgame, and sometimes it's the

LIST OF SUBSTITUTES (SOME WITH TOLL-FREE NUMBERS)

IN-LAW VISITING SCHEDULE

POSSIBLY THE LESSON BOOK?

AIRLINE TICKETS

FOR FAMILY MEDICAL CRISES

SARA SURROGATE

headache she gets when she "overdoes." Every now and then one of Sara's children has a virus, and that causes her to miss Sunday school.

Sara does make an effort to get to Sunday school whenever she can. That is, if there's not a tennis tournament that her son is playing in or a special weekend get-away trip planned by her bridge club. If she doesn't have to stay up too late on Saturday night waiting for her teenagers to get in, or if she doesn't feel the need to visit her parents out of town, she'll make it to Sunday school.

Sara usually manages to find a substitute for herself when she will be absent, but she frequently doesn't do it until the very last minute. If there is no time to get a lesson book to the substitute, she just instructs, "Oh, you can tell them a story or something." There are some story records and a record player in Sara's classroom that she usually tells the substitutes to rely on. The kids in the class know the stories backwards by now.

Sara finds her substitutes in a number of places. Sometimes she sends her teenage daughter or one of her daughter's friends to "hold down the fort." Sara is happy to use anyone who is willing to fill in for her; whether or not that person knows anything about children or Sunday school is immaterial.

There are Sundays when Sara cannot find a substitute. When that happens, she calls the church on Sunday morning and asks whoever answers the phone to leave a note on her classroom door telling the kids to go into the first and second grade class or the fifth and sixth grade class — whichever they choose. In doing so, she succeeds in ruining all three classes that day.

Needless to say, there is no continuity, unit plan, or overall direction in Sara's class. The children are not well behaved, and they usually try to play sneaky little tricks on Sara when she does come. They think she is a substitute teacher.

LAST MINUTE LIZ

You can count on Last Minute Liz. She's at Sunday school every Sunday — about ten minutes after it's supposed to start.

Liz always blows into the room like a typhoon, one curler still in her hair, her last button undone, her Sunday school book still in the car, and an excuse on her lips.

LIST OF
EXCUSES
(CHECK ONE)

LAST MINUTE LIZ

The reasons for Liz's tardiness are varied and endless. Either the alarm clock didn't ring, the bathtub overflowed, or the dog threw up on the carpet, and it would have left a stain if she hadn't taken time to clean it up.

Sometimes she runs out of gas. Occasionally she has a flat tire. Every now and then the car won't start. Frequently she can't find the car keys.

But it's usually not Liz's fault. It's her family that causes the trouble. Her husband insists on reading the Sunday paper before Sunday school, and her kids dawdle and piddle around, endlessly twisting their socks and rearranging the toothpaste on the end of the toothbrush.

Liz teaches first and second graders. Some of the younger ones don't like to be left in the Sunday school room with no teacher, so their parents hang around until Liz arrives. That makes the parents late for their classes.

Before Liz gets there, older boys pick on younger ones, shy kids cower in the corner, and hyperactive youngsters swing from the light fixtures.

It takes a while for Liz to get herself together, calm the class down, and get started on the lesson. There's seldom time to take advantage of the many activities suggested in the teacher's book. Most of them require paper, paint, scissors, glue, crayons, or other supplies that Liz can't seem to locate. Sometimes she pokes through the cabinets that belong to the weekday kindergarten in hopes of finding some art and craft supplies, but the kids usually get into so much mischief while she's looking that it's hardly worth the effort. By the time she has marked the roll, told a story and sung a song or two, it's time for the bell. Liz always dismisses the class right on time.

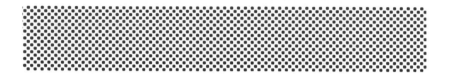

How To Get To Sunday School On Time:

1. Fill car with gas and check tires Saturday afternoon.
2. Study your Sunday school lesson all week and review on Saturday afternoon.
3. Cook Sunday dinner Saturday.
4. Lay out all Sunday clothes Saturday night. (Buttons and hems intact, wrinkles pressed, shoes shined.)
5. Bathe and shampoo Saturday night.
6. Go to bed at 8:30 Saturday night.
7. Set three alarm clocks. Put one in an aluminum pan so it will make more noise.
8. Skip breakfast Sunday morning.
9. Cancel your subscription to the Sunday paper.
10. Chloroform your family.

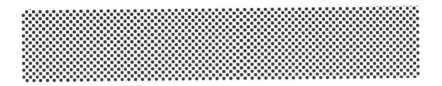

Appropriate Gifts Children Can Give Sunday School Teachers:

1. Peanut butter covered pinecone on a string (makes excellent bird feeder).
2. Panty hose (to replace those torn on the little wooden chairs at Sunday school).
3. Chalk.
4. One perfect rose.
5. One perfect BMW.
6. Jewlery box made from hand-painted cigar box.
7. Two carat diamond ring to put in jewelry box.
8. Construction paper place mats.
9. Full length mink coat.
10. A copy of *The Official Sunday School Handbook.*

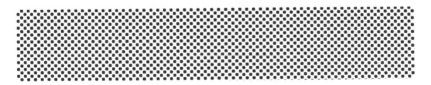

NANCY NERVOUS

Nancy Nervous anticipates her Sunday school class like most folks anticipate taking up residence in a nursing home. She dreads dealing with those little monsters who wiggle and giggle and drive her up the wall. She thinks they are a bunch of self-centered attention-getters whose sole purpose in this world is making her Sunday mornings miserable.

The more the kids misbehave, the more nervous Nancy gets. She doesn't understand why they don't just sit quietly and listen to the Sunday school lesson. Nancy has explained to them that she doesn't like noise, but they are still noisy.

Nancy would not dare tackle some of the activities suggested in the curriculum materials. The very idea of getting involved with paint, modeling clay, or glue puts her in a nervous jerk. It's not only the clutter of craft projects that upsets Nancy, it's that the kids move around and make noise when they work on those projects, and Nancy can't stand confusion. The kids bump into each other, scrape their chairs on the floor, and end up in all sorts of unpredictable positions. Besides, what if someone spilled something? What if a kid put clay up his nose? What if they all got tetanus from the scissors?

Nancy likes orderliness, neatness, predictability, precision and attention to detail. She has a carefully scheduled lesson plan, and she gets in a tizzy if anyone interrupts or delays it.

Nancy does not encourage questions. Not only do they take up time and get her off schedule, but she is terrified that someone will ask her something she can't answer. She studies the lesson and tries to understand all the points that should be made, but she gets very tense just thinking about what some kid might want her to explain.

A large percentage of class time is devoted to reminding the children that they are in church and should therefore behave like little ladies and little gentlemen. Sometimes Nancy tries to control the seven-year-olds by explaining to them that her life is full of stress and that she has had a very rough week. She doesn't understand why these talks never seem to do any good. The kids continue to be too noisy and active to suit Nancy.

It worries Nancy that she thinks about child abuse laws so much. It bothers her that she is tempted every Sunday morning to rely on tranquilizers to get her through the lesson. But then it also worries her that a tree could fall on the church, lightning could strike the steeple, the piano in the classroom

CRAFT SUPPLIES

TIMER FOR LESSONS

EAR PLUGS

RICHTER SCALE

NANCY NERVOUS

125

above could fall through the ceiling, or the water fountain could explode.

CHILDREN AND SUNDAY SCHOOL

If you don't like kids, do them and yourself a favor, and don't teach them in Sunday school. Like dogs and horses, children sense how you feel about them.

Most teachers are never completely satisified with their teaching. Most think they could have done a better job on any given lesson. But if teachers never have a feeling of joyful satisfaction in their teaching, if they never get personal enjoyment from being with their students, then the students probably don't like the teaching-learning situation either, and more than likely, they find very little meaning in it.

Teachers who are constantly annoyed or frustrated with class members had better look at their teaching procedures. They should be sure they understand the normal nature and characteristics of children. Those characteristics determine children's needs and how they learn. The way in which children learn should determine how we go about trying to teach them.

Kids Aren't Grownups, But They Are People

Children are not miniature adults, so they should not be expected to think and act like adults. But they do have this in common with adults — they are all individuals with their own sets of uniquely combined genes and their own spots in the world that no one else can fit or fill. Children need teachers who will make the effort to get to know each one as an individual. Teachers who are able to plan effectively for their students must know the kids and their particular needs, problems, abilities, limitations and family situations. They need to take into account the individual personalities of class members — the shy ones, the hyperactive ones, the slow ones, the bright ones.

Kids Aren't Monsters, But Sometimes You Wonder

Although no two children are alike, there are characteristics of each group of which teachers should be aware. Younger elementary children are as full of energy as a nuclear power plant. They are noisy, restless, messy and extremely active. They can't help being self-centered. They were made that way. They aren't beasts; they are children.

Young children are curious, so they explore, investigate and take things apart. They have countless questions about every conceivable subject, and they usually believe whatever adults tell them.

It's impossible for kids to sit still and listen for a very long time. Their short attention span and need for movement are normal for their age. The reason they do not sit still and pay attention for any length of time is that their bodies are not yet ready to do that. They learn best through their own purposeful activity. They learn more from what they do than from what they hear.

Successful teachers take advantage of these characteristics by providing plenty of activities that allow children to participate as fully as possible. They make provisions for exploring, experimenting and investigating. They go with the flow when things seem messy and noisy. But they also realize that even children cannot operate in constant noise and chaos. They too need moments of quiet and order— a time for a story, a worship experience, a prayer. The trick is to alternate active, busy times with quiet times. No one can tolerate pandemonium indefinitely.

Things Do Get Better Or Worse

As children grow into older elementary years, they have different characteristics. They can sit still and concentrate for longer periods of time.

ELEMENTARY CHILDREN ARE FULL OF ENERGY

They are able to organize and carry through a prolonged activity or project. They are increasingly independent, enjoy perfecting their skills, and want to make their own decisions. They like to be involved with the teacher in making plans for class activities. Teachers need to allow for this by remaining open-minded and planning with the class instead of for it. Unlike Nancy Nervous, teachers can have a lesson plan without being a slave to it. Schedules should be flexible enough to allow for unexpected developments.

Older elementary boys and girls can think abstractly and reason in a way that would have been impossible to them earlier. They feel intensely about fairness, and they are more skeptical, often questioning things they had accepted before. They have serious questions that really concern them, and they don't want glib answers. They can spot phoniness and see through insincerity.

Teachers should be willing to admit that they don't know all the answers. A teacher's attitude in dealing with a question is more important than the number of answers the teacher knows. It's more helpful for a teacher to show genuine interest and concern for the student than to be a walking encyclopedia or Bible commentary. Nevertheless, good teachers are eager to study and help students find answers.

During the years of older childhood, peer pressure rears its head. What "the gang" thinks is extremely important. Older children look to their contemporaries rather than adults for authority, and they have a tendency to accept the values of the group without question.

This is the time when thousands of children are introduced to drugs and alcohol. Drug and alcohol abuse take place among elementary age children as well as teens and adults. Parents and teachers must not wait until the teenage years to educate youth about these dangers. Many sixth graders are already addicted.

Teachers can help youngsters through the older elementary years by providing wholesome, meaningful activities in a group in which the kids can feel accepted. Older children need a sense of belonging, and they need encouragement to do things within a group whose values are desirable.

Teachers cannot impose a set of values upon a child, but they can provide the means by which a child can develop his or her own set of values. Likewise, teachers cannot prescribe the nature of a child's response to God, but they can create an environment and situation in which a child can come to know God.

Children Learn Through Relationships

Whether it's the younger elementary child or the older one, the teacher's primary responsibility is relating to the child. Children learn through relationships as much as they do through a planned lesson. Learning through relationships takes place whether it is intended or not; it takes place through verbal and non-verbal communication. When teachers treat children with dignity, love, acceptance, understanding and respect, they build a foundation for self-understanding and acceptance that makes it possible for children to come to see themselves as people who are loved, accepted and forgiven by God.

Beautiful spacious rooms, top-notch teaching equipment and excellent curriculum materials are all important and desirable. But none of those things are adequate substitutes for the relationship between teacher and student.

THERE IS NO SUBSTITUTE FOR A
GOOD RELATIONSHIP BETWEEN
TEACHER AND STUDENTS

Relationships Need Continuity

In order for a teacher-pupil relationship to be established, children need to see the same teacher at Sunday school every Sunday. With teachers like Sara Surrogate, how can a child learn dependability and trust? How can a teacher lay a foundation and build on it? Because teachers are human beings who walk around in bodies and live in families, they will, no doubt, have to be absent from time to time. But insofar as possible, they should teach every Sunday for several consecutive months. A year is preferable. Don't rotate Sunday by Sunday. That destroys continuity and makes relating to children in a meaningful way almost impossible.

When it is necessary to call in a substitute, that person should know the children and be familiar with the literature and class procedure. Every teacher deserves to have a reliable, competent substitute to call on in a pinch.

When The Going Gets Tough

No matter how much you love them — no matter how hard you try — no matter how adorable you think the kids are — there are times when you'd like to jerk them up by the hair of the head and toss them into the black hole.

Nobody ever said it would be easy. But what do you do when there is so much misbehavior that you feel more like you're in reform school than Sunday school?

Remember that there's a reason for everything people do, including acting obnoxious at Sunday school. Try to discover the reason behind behavior rather than merely attacking the behavior directly.

Be consistent. Kids get confused when the rules keep changing, so make sure everyone knows what is acceptable and what is unacceptable. If it was out of bounds last Sunday, it's out of bounds every Sunday. Rest assured they'll test the boundaries to see how far they can go.

The Latin word that gives us *discipline* also gives us *disciple*. Both words have to do with learning. Try to see discipline as a learning experience rather than punishment.

Children who feel loved usually want to please those who love them. In dealing with misbehavior, let the child know that it is the action that is unacceptable, not the child. Just as God loves us no matter what we do, we love the child, no matter what he or she does. But we do not love misbehavior, and we do not tolerate misbehavior.

Sometimes discipline problems can be avoided by simply getting the day off to a good start. This is possible only if the teacher arrives at Sunday school before the children do. If there is a smiling, loving teacher waiting to greet children as they arrive, if the teacher is in a happy, positive frame of mind, and if the teacher has plenty of interesting, challenging activities planned for the children to begin work on immediately, the little ones are not very likely to get into any mischief.

Discipline problems should be handled lovingly, tactfully, fairly, promptly, briefly and definitely. One of our purposes is teaching self-control, and we do that best by exhibiting self-control. Flying off the handle in a fit of rage won't do the trick.

Prevention works best. Keep them busy. Keep them interested. Keep them curious. Keep them challenged. Keep them doing things at which they can feel successful. Keep them involved in planning their own activities. That'll usually keep them out of trouble.

KEEP THEM DOING THINGS AT WHICH THEY CAN FEEL SUCCESSFUL

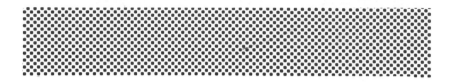

Answers To Questions You Don't Know The Answers To:

1. Open your mouth one more time, and I'll wash it out with soap.
2. Didn't your mother ever tell you that children are to be seen and not heard?
3. If I tell you, it will only confuse you.
4. God planned it that way. (Only works with "why?" questions.)
5. I was just about to assign that question to the entire class for homework. Yes, you certainly can give homework in Sunday school.
6. You ask too many questions.
7. No speaky de English.
8. In order to answer that, I'd have to outline it on the board, and since I'm out of chalk, you're out of luck.
9. I've just been afflicted with an acute case of amnesia.
10. I don't know, but let's find out together.

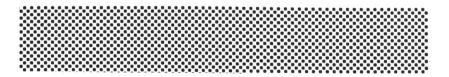

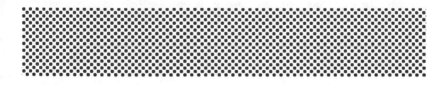

Questions Sunday School Teachers Wish Kids Wouldn't Ask:

1. How did Noah keep all the animals on the ark from eating each other up?
2. Will my pet gerbil go to heaven?
3. Do you believe in evolution?
4. How could a woman be turned into a block of salt?
5. Why did Jesus curse the fig tree?
6. What is circumcision?
7. My step-father is Jewish. Will he go to heaven?
8. Do you believe in interracial marriage?
9. My mother says it's wrong to drink. So why did Jesus make wine for that wedding?
10. How did Noah feed all the animals on the ark?

HOW TO USE A LESSON PLAN

Sunday school teachers don't have to be like Nancy Nervous in order to use a lesson plan. The secret is to use the plan instead of letting the plan use you. A lesson plan is a self-imposed guideline, so if you don't stick to the schedule minute by minute, that's okay. You are not planning a lesson — you are planning *for* a lesson. Remain flexible so that you can meet the interests and needs of the students.

Going through the process of writing out a lesson plan forces you to clarify in your own mind what you hope will be accomplished and how you intend to help class members accomplish it. Remember, you're not the one who will accomplish it. You can't impose learning on your class or even transmit it to them. They will have to do their own learning. You will set the stage and provide the environment.

Begin by writing the titles of the unit and lesson. Writing the words reinforces in your mind what the lesson is about. There is probably a stated purpose for every lesson in the quarterly. Try paraphrasing the purpose to make yourself think about it.

Don't leave anything blank on your lesson plan. Even if you assume you know what you will do or how you will arrange the room, write it down anyway. List every supply and resource you plan to use.

Invest in a pocket looseleaf notebook in which you can keep your quarterly, teacher's manual, rollbook and lesson plans. Duplicate fifty-two copies of a lesson plan form. (Look at the one on page 136 for an idea, but make your own form to suit your particular needs and procedures.) Date a lesson plan form for every Sunday in the year. If you plan to be absent, be sure to get that Sunday's form to your substitute and ask him or her to return it to you after the session.

Don't dispose of the lesson plan form after Sunday school is over. Use it to write an evaluation of the session while it is still fresh in your mind. List activities that were especially successful, as well as those that didn't work out. Make a notation of teaching methods that need improvement. Looking over the evaluations from time to time will help in future planning.

Use your Sunday school notebook to jot down ideas to try in the future. Keep a list in it of supplies or resources you need to get, and use it to make notations about class members who need a visit or phone call.

AFTER EACH CLASS, USE THE LESSON PLAN FORM FOR WRITING AN EVALUATION OF HOW IT WENT

Plan carefully and specifically, but don't be a slave to your plans. As experiences develop within the group, you may want to depart from your outline. That's fine. The students are more important than the schedule.

LESSON PLANS		
DATE:		
UNIT TITLE:		
LESSON TITLE:		
LESSON PURPOSE:		
SCRIPTURE:		
APPROX. TIME	ACTIVITY	MATERIALS, EQUIPMENT, RESOURCES
ROOM ARRANGEMENT:		
EVALUATION:		

Sunday School Sue

dear sunday skool sue,

im just a litel kid and some groan peepul dont pay much attenshun to me but i hurd you like for peepul to rite to you about sunday skool so im writing.

i like sunday skool and i love my sunday skool teechur. i want to be like my sunday skool teechur becuz she is happy and she looks purty. she treets me like im important so i no she loves me and she tells me what is true. my teechur says god loves me so i no he does and i love god.

my teechur is kind and gentel and talks softly. why do some teechurs talk loud and tell the kids to talk quiet? my teechur nos that i cant be still very long. she gives me lots of chances to move arounnd and do difrent things in sunday skool.

there are some things i can do and some things i cant do. when i can do it my teechur lets me do it but when i cant she helps me. but she does not do it for me if i can do it for myself. i like that.

sometimes i get angree. my teechur stops me before i hurt anyone. im glad she does becuz i realy dont want to hurt peepul. i need her to watch me and help me becuz im stil litel and sometimes i dont do the best thing.

i have important work to do at sunday skool. i need to paint and draw and make things and figur things out. my teechur lets me work and she nos what im doing is importunt.

my teechur nos that i get embarassed ezily. she never puts me on the spot in front of my friends or makes me look stupid or bad. she is payshunt and tackful when she korreks me. im glad of that. she says jesus was kind. she must

137

*be a lot like jesus. im only seven now but when
i get groan up im gonna marry her.*

a litel kid

Dear Little Kid:

   **Your Sunday school teacher may not
still be your choice for a wife when you grow
up. Besides she will probably be married
already. But if you can still remember to
send her a love letter when you're tall and
20 I'm sure it would make her very happy.**

Sunday School Sue

**P.S. I think her husband would under-
stand.**

Chapter 8:
HOW INNOCENT IS A SUNDAY SCHOOL PICNIC?
Where there's Smoke there's Marshmallows

L et's hear it for the Sunday school picnic! Where else in today's world can you find a party at which the only chemical substance is insect repellent?

With the surge of nostalgia that has swept the country in recent years, the old-fashioned Sunday school picnic has enjoyed resurrection from its premature death. Once again parents, children, aunts, uncles, neighbors and friends gather for binges of eating, volleyball and three-legged races.

THE SUNDAY SCHOOL PICNIC

Sunday School Sue

Dear Sunday School Sue,

Every year at our Sunday school picnic, people bring scrumptuous casseroles, salads, sandwiches, cakes and pies. The food always appears to be more than adequate for an army. But the kids run ahead and get at the front of the line. They must think they're supposed to take some of everything that's there, because they fill their plates with more than a lumberjack could eat. By the time the adults get to serve themselves, the desserts are crumbs, the sandwiches have disappeared, and there's nothing left but a limp pickle or two. Most of what was on the kids' plates ends up in the garbage. Any suggestions?

Hungry in Houston

Dear Hungry,

There are several possible solutions to your problem. You could request that everyone bring spinach, broccoli or brussels sprouts. Or you could see to it that the tables are five feet high. Maybe it would be easier just to tie the kids to a tree until all adults are served. Or ask whoever says the blessing to announce that all children are to report to their parents immediately so families can go through the serving line together.

Sunday School Sue

Dear Sunday School Sue,

I'm tired of the usual fare that we have at our Sunday school picnic. Food is getting so expensive these days, and there's always such a huge crowd to feed at these gatherings, that I'm wondering if it's worth the trouble to cook all that food and take it to the picnic. If I had a good recipe for an economical dish that would serve a large crowd, I wouldn't mind making it. Do you have any ideas?

Stumped in Savannah

Dear Stumped,

Here's just what you need to feed your hungry crowd.

RHINOCEROS STEW:

Ingredients:
  1 rhinoceros
  3 rabbits, optional
  salt and pepper to taste
  gravy (lots)

Cut rhinoceros into bite size pieces. (Reserve the horn so you can call everyone when it's ready.) Cover with gravy and simmer for a month. Serves 2,475. If you need to stretch it, add the rabbits, but do this only in an emergency, because most people do not like to find "hare" in their stew.

EVERYBODY LOVES A PICNIC

The old-fashioned picnic has a new twist. It is no longer limited to the Sunday school, but it has become a church-wide function for most congregations. The picnic can be as simple as dinner on the grounds in small rural churches to elaborate barbeques in the suburbs or overnight camp-outs sponsored by large metropolitan churches.

Whether the picnic is held in a city park, the church's back yard, or a cow pasture, this great congregational gathering could be used to celebrate and boost the Sunday school. There are several ways to do that.

141

Ask each Sunday school class to help provide the entertainment after the meal. Stress that as many class members as possible should participate. Entertainment should be simple, light and fun. It can be a song sung by the entire class, a few jokes told by several class members, or a silly skit performed by the group.

All classes, young and old, should participate. A kitchen gadget band would be fun for the ladies' class, and a comic fashion show (men in women's clothes) would be hilarious for the men's class.

There are plenty of funny skits available that youth and adult classes could perform. Most of these skits take very little rehearsal and less talent.

The entertainment could include, but not be limited to, special performances by class members who have outstanding talents in music, dance or drama. However, if there are several really talented performers, they might discourage others who are not so gifted. The idea is not to showcase talent but to encourage participation for everyone's fun.

Having all Sunday school classes involved in the entertainment will not only enhance the feeling of camaraderie in the classes, it will be good advertisement for each group. Those at the picnic who don't attend Sunday school will probably knock the door down to get there when they see how much fun Sunday school folks can have.

A Little Competition Can Be A Lot Of Fun

Another way to highlight the Sunday school at a church-wide picnic is to have classes compete against one another in silly contests. Careful planning will be necessary to ensure that classes that compete are evenly matched. Also be sure the contest fits the age group that participates in it. Use your imagination to come up with ridiculous ways to compete, or use some of the following tried and true contests.

INNER TUBE RELAY RACE: Squeeze as many people as possible inside an automobile inner tube. Use one tube per team. The first group runs to the finish line, returns to its team members, removes the inner tube, and gives it to the next group to squeeze into and race. The strategy is to figure out whether it takes more time to squeeze another person in or to make more trips to the finish line.

BUBBLE GUM BLOWING CONTEST: Every contestant

MAKE SURE THE COMPETITORS ARE EVENLY MATCHED

gets a paper plate that contains a piece of bubble gum hidden under a plate full of flour. Team members must hold the paper plate with both hands. They are not allowed to touch the bubble gum with their hands. They must blow the flour away until they find the bubble gum, and then get the gum into their mouths without using their hands. The first one who can chew the gum and blow a bubble wins.

CRACKER-WHISTLE CONTEST: Place five crackers on a paper plate. No hands allowed. The team member who can eat all the crackers and whistle first is the winner.

OVER-UNDER WATER RELAY: Each team stands in line, facing forward. There is a bucket of water at the beginning of the line and an empty bucket at the end of the line. The object is to fill the empty bucket with water from the full bucket. The first team member fills a cup with water from the bucket and then passes it over his head (without turning around). The next one must pass the cup of water under — between his legs — without turning around. The over and under procedure continues until the last person in line empties the cup of water into the bucket. The cup is then passed over and under back to the front of the line where it is refilled, and starts its journey again. The team that fills its bucket first wins.

SPOON AND BOTTLE WATER RELAY: This is a variation of the above game, except a spoon and bottle are used.

WILLIAM TELL'S WATER PISTOL CONTEST: Half the team members sit with empty paper cups on their heads. The other team members stand behind the boundry line, facing those with cups on their heads, and try to fill the cups with water by shooting it from their water pistols. When all water pistols are empty, water from the cups of each team is poured up and measured. The team with the most water wins.

BALLOON RELAY: Each team member is given a balloon. At the signal, the first team member blows up his balloon, ties it off, places the balloon between his knees, runs to the goal line, (if he drops the balloon from between his knees, he starts over). When he touches the goal line, he places the balloon on the ground, and steps on it until it pops. He then runs back and tags the next team member who blows up his balloon, ties it off, runs to the goal, and so forth. The first team to pop all its balloons wins.

OLD FAVORITE RELAYS: Relay races that have been enjoyed at Sunday school picnics down through the years include passing a Life Saver down the line on a toothpick held between the teeth, and passing an orange down the line from underneath one chin to underneath the next chin. Then there's the potato-between-the-knees relay, the egg-in-a-spoon relay, and the push-a-peanut-with-your-nose relay. There are sack races, three-legged races, hold-the-frisbee-between-two-sets-of-hips races, obstacle course relays, and many others. Relays are good entertainment at Sunday school picnics because they provide maximum participation.

The daring souls at the Sunday school picnic may want to try the greased pole climb, the water balloon toss, and the egg toss. Others might prefer a yo-yo contest, hoola hoop contest, frisbee throw or bobbing for apples. Don't think these games are limited to kids. Adults who get into the spirit of the occasion can have a good time, and the children will be delighted that the adults "got down on their level" for once.

It's fun to play kick-ball or frisbee using softball rules, and then there are always the old stand-bys for group recreation, volleyball and dodge ball.

Check your church or public library for books that describe group games. Remember to choose games that are difficult enough to be challenging, but not so difficult that they discourage participation.

Plan something for everyone. Younger children should have special games set up just for them. Little ones don't under-

KIDS LIKE TO SEE ADULTS "COME DOWN TO THEIR LEVEL"

stand about winning and losing, so have games that encourage participation rather than competition for pre-schoolers.

Build A Bonfire

Unless your church picnic is held on a hot summer afternoon, build a bonfire so kids can toast marshmallows and have something to sit around for the sing-along and vespers that will probably follow the picnic. In case there's anyone out there who was raised on Venus, here's the recipe for the all time favorite bonfire treat.

S'MORES: Place a toasted marshmallow and a piece of chocolate bar between two graham crackers.

BETTER THAN S'MORES: Cover two saltine crackers with peanut butter. Place a toasted marshmallow between them.

Banana Split In A Rain Gutter:

If you try the following idea at your Sunday school picnic, be sure to spread the word beforehand that no one should bring dessert.

Go to a building supply business and borrow a section of rain gutter at least 20-feet long. Wash the gutter thoroughly, line it with aluminum foil, and place it on long picnic tables. Get several people to help you build a 20-foot banana split. It takes several workers, because if you do it alone, you'll still be peeling bananas, and the ice cream will have melted. Fill the

145

gutter with different flavors of ice cream. Add bananas, chocolate syrup, whipped cream, cherries, nuts and whatever else tempts your tummy. While you and your assistants are assembling the sinful concoction, have someone distribute plastic spoons to the crowd. When the whistle blows, everyone can make a dive for a place at the table and dig in. The crowd will never forget the experience.

SALMONELLA SALLY

Salmonella Sally loves to cook. She takes great pride in arriving at every Sunday school picnic carrying an enormous picnic basket filled with her favorite dishes. Her old-fashioned basket is festooned with red and white ribbons, and it's lined in colorful gingham.

In Sally's oversized hamper there are always deviled eggs, fried chicken, potato salad, cole slaw, turkey salad sandwiches, egg custard and coconut cake. Every year Sally slaves in her kitchen for three days to prepare the beautiful feast.

All of the dishes that Sally prepares look so pretty arranged on the kitchen counter. They are displayed there for several hours before the picnic so that anyone who happens to drop by can see how hard Sally has worked and how much she is taking to "spread."

Sally thinks that food as scrumptious looking as hers deserves a place of honor on the picnic table. To ensure this, Sally always arrives at the picnic early and sees to it that her food is placed in a convenient and conspicuous spot. So it's usually another hour before her food is eaten.

SALMONELLA SALLY

It would never occur to Sally that the peculiar stomach virus that went around the night of last year's Sunday school picnic had anything at all to do with her delicious food. Sally would be highly insulted if anyone suggested such a thing. After all, everyone knows Sally is one of the best cooks in the county!

Handling Food At A Picnic

It wouldn't be a picnic without all those traditional picnic foods that Salmonella Sally loves to prepare, and there's no reason why folks can't enjoy them without getting food poisoning.

If someone could only convince Sally that delicious, perfectly prepared foods can develop toxins, maybe she would be willing to refrigerate her tempting treats.

There are several things Sally could do to make her food as safe as it is attractive and tasty. She could make her sandwiches the day before and freeze them. By taking them out of the freezer and placing them in her picnic basket shortly before time for the big event, she would allow plenty of time for them to thaw, but not enough time for them to develop toxins.

Sally should use that pretty basket for frozen sandwiches, potato chips, paper plates, cups and napkins. All of her other food should be kept in an ice chest so that it remains cold.

Life Begins At Forty

That cliché should remind Salmonella Sally that some foods that are above 40° for a couple of hours can cause food poisoning. To avoid trouble, a good rule of thumb is **keep hot foods hot and cold foods cold.** It's the in-between temperatures that are dangerous. To help keep food hot, wrap the dishes in many layers of paper or reheat them if there is a fire at the picnic. It's better to take uncooked weiners in an ice chest or cooler and then cook them on the spot.

Not all foods will develop Salmonella toxins, but those Sally likes to take are prime candidates for the problem. Poultry, dairy products and anything containing eggs should be kept cold.

Things you can count on not to give you food poisoning are pre-packaged snack foods and fresh fruit. And if you don't like to cook, it's nice to say that avoiding Salmonella poisoning is the reason you always bring potato chips and apples to the Sunday school picnic.

Vespers

Many Sunday school picnics conclude with vespers. A brief worship service is an appropriate way to end a happy day of playing, eating and visiting.

A campfire is a perfect spot for the service. If that is not possible, choose a place that is quiet and especially pretty.

The vesper service can provide another opportunity to highlight the Sunday school. Each class could be responsible for leading a section of the service. Children's classes could present a special hymn or choral reading. Members of youth classes could lead in prayer, and representatives from adult classes could share devotional thoughts. It's important that someone plan and coordinate the service in advance in order to maintain a worshipful and reverent atmosphere and keep

LET EACH CLASS LEAD A SECTION OF THE
VESPER SERVICE

things moving smoothly.

Make sure that arrangements have been made for adequate lighting if the service continues after nightfall. Children, young people and some adults will not mind sitting on the ground, but be sure to provide folding chairs for elderly adults.

Someone should be designated to distribute hymnbooks and collect them after the service. If you decide to have a candlelight service, make the necessary arrangements well in advance.

Keep the worship program brief. It will have been a long and tiring day, and people will not want to sit on the ground for more than a few minutes. Remember that there will probably be many small children in attendance, so keep them in mind in your planning.

Some appropriate themes for such an outdoor vesper service are the beauty of God's creation, stewardship of the earth, and the value of Christian fellowship.

HELPFUL RESOURCES FOR YOUR SUNDAY SCHOOL PICNIC AND WHERE TO FIND THEM

GAMES: Need more ideas for games? If you can't find books of games and recreation ideas in your church or public library, here are some you can order:

The New Games Book, by Andrew Fluegelman *(Doubleday)*

More New Games, by Andrew Fluegelman *(Doubleday/ Dolphin)*

Vol. 1 - Games: The New Fun Encyclopedia, by E. O. Harbin, *revised and updated by Bob Sessoms*

Order from: *Discipleship Resources*
P.O. Box 189
Nashville, TN 37202

SKITS: For group entertainment nothing beats the fun of skits. For catalogs full of them, write to:

Contemporary Drama Service
885 Elkton Drive
Colorado Springs, CO 80907

SONG BOOKS: For singing around the campfire or any sing-along time, here are some appropriate songbooks:

Singing The Lord's Song
Order from: *Discipleship Resources*
P.O. Box 189
Nashville, TN 37202

50 Folk Favorites
Bus Sing
Youth Favorites

Order from: *Zondervan Corp.*
1415 Lake Dr., S.E.
Grand Rapids, MI 49506

Chapter 9:
PREVAILING WITH PRE-SCHOOLERS

MARY MIGHTY-MOM

The baby was up half the night with colic. When Mary Mighty-Mom finally got him to sleep and was resting soundly in her own bed, the four-year-old called her to come find him some dry, clean sheets and pajamas. When the bed and child were changed and Mary fast asleep, her six-year-old woke her crying, "I dreamed there was this big green monster on a motorcycle, and it's in my closet, and can I sleep with you and Daddy?" So Mary was kneed and elbowed the rest of the night. Perhaps because it was Sunday, the two-year-old slept late. She didn't scream for Mary until 6 a.m.

MARY MIGHTY-MOM

Bleary-eyed, Mary re-read her Sunday school lesson between spoonsful of oatmeal, and she mentally reviewed her lesson plan as she whipped up a meatloaf, congealed salad, and dump cake for Sunday dinner. After she cleaned the jelly from the carpet, mopped up the spilled milk, wiped three noses, settled two arguments and found the lost turtle, Mary did the dishes, thanked the Lord that everything was going so well that morning and started getting the kids dressed.

Mary has never understood why Sunday mornings are so much more difficult than week days. Every day she gets her husband off to work, the six-year-old on the school bus and the four-year-old ready for kindergarten, all while tending to the two-year-old and baby. But there's something about getting the whole family fed and dressed for Sunday school that is overwhelming.

Why is Sunday morning always crisis time? If a kid gets his head stuck between the stairway bannisters, it's on Sunday morning. Shoes that are in the middle of the living room floor all week long, mysteriously disappear on Sunday morning. Why is it always Sunday morning when there's a power outage? Boys who decide to paint the cat with shoe polish, do so on Sunday morning. Toddlers who lock themselves in the bathroom with the water running full force do it on Sunday morning. Murphy's Law was discovered on Sunday morning.

Sometimes Mary wonders if she's the right one for the kindergarten Sunday school class she teaches. She is so exhausted by the time she gets to Sunday school that it takes every ounce of self-discipline she can muster to be civil, much less patient, kind and understanding.

Mary tries to get to Sunday school early because she knows she should cheerfully greet the children in her class. But in order for her to go early, her entire family must also go early. Usually teachers in the other classrooms have not arrived to look after Mary's kids while Mary is busy preparing to look after someone else's kids. If it weren't for her husband, she'd never make it. He quietly helps out, all the time thinking that he'd rather be reading the Sunday paper.

When Mary gets really tired, she resents being the one in charge of the kindergarten class. But then she loves kids, and she knows that it's not easy to get people to teach Sunday school. She just wonders if she shouldn't be getting some help from those parents who are dropping their kids off at Sunday school and then going out for a quiet, adult breakfast buffet.

Teachers In The Preschool Department

Why is it that mothers who spend their entire week dealing with preschoolers end up teaching them in Sunday school as well? If there is anyone in the world who needs the intellectual stimulation, intelligent conversation and physical inactivity that takes place in an adult Sunday school class, it's people like Mary Mighty-Mom. There ought to be a law that prohibits women with a house full of preschoolers from spending their Sunday mornings with anyone under 18.

There also ought to be a law that prohibits sexual discrimination in preschool teacher recruitment. Men need to share in the joys and rewards of working with little ones. Whoever said only women could keep the nursery or teach toddlers? Now that mommies are in the work force in increasing numbers, daddies all over the land are proving how capable they are as care-givers. The preschool department provides a marvelous opportunity for the church to teach by example that Christians are not bound by outdated sexual stereotypes. Because so many households are headed by women today and because men are so frequently absent from the home for business reasons, young children more than ever need to spend time with men. Boys not only need male role models, but all children need to see men in a role that is loving, caring and sensitive. Children need to hear men pray and talk about God. If preschoolers see and hear only women in Sunday school, they might think that Christianity is limited to females.

By the way, nobody ever said you have to be a parent to teach in the preschool department.

Sunday School Sue

Dear Sunday School Sue,

I often wonder what is going on in the adult Sunday school classes. I've forgotten what it's like to participate in a worship service. I long to hear an inspiring sermon and join the congregation in singing praises to God. People tell me we have an excellent choir now, and I hear that the preacher's pretty good. But how should I know.?

You think I'm a shut-in? Does it sound like I'm forced to work at a Sunday job? Guess again. I'm at church every Sunday morning, but instead of participating in the worship service or attending an adult Sunday school class, I'm stuck in the nursery.

Don't get me wrong, I love the kids, and they seem to like me. I was happy to accept the job when I was asked to take it four years ago. However, there are some disadvantages. In addition to missing out on Bible study, sermons and worship experiences, I'm not meeting the new people who are joining our church unless they happen to have a baby. There are people in our congregation who see me during the week and say, "We've been missing you at church. Why did you stop coming?" Not only that, but every time I wear a new dress, some baby spits up on it.

Am I terribly selfish? What is your recommendation?

Tired in Tampa

Dear Tired,

No, you're not selfish. Sounds like you're

157

suffering from what nearly all nursery workers get from time to time — baby burnout. Four years is three years too long for anyone to serve in the nursery. Turn in your notice, tell them you mean business, get back into an adult Sunday school class, and start participating in the worship service again. Fair is fair.

In a couple of years, if you miss those babies, volunteer for the nursery again. But get it in writing that you're only in for a one-year hitch.

Sunday School Sue

Dear Sunday School Sue,

You won't believe what happened in my kindergarten class this morning. A precious little newcomer visited — I think her family just moved to town from Arkansas. The four-year-old was all dressed up in a ruffled outfit, and she had the prettiest blond curls you ever saw.

About halfway through the "cut and paste" period, I looked up just in time to see one of the five-year-old boys take the scissors and clip off a beautiful blond ringlet from the visitor's hair.

I was so mortified I hid in the bathroom when the little girl's parents came to pick her up. What must I do about this?

Mortified in Minneapolis

Dear Mortified,

You probably won't get an opportunity to do anything about it, because these folks will more than likely never darken the door of your church again.

Many young couples who move to a new town choose a church largely on the basis of what it offers their children. They expect a safe, well-equipped and properly supervised environment as well as meaningful educational and spiritual guidance for the little ones. A young family's first impression of the church often comes from the preschool department. In this case, the first im-

158

pression needs to be corrected. Maybe you could find out who these people are and call to explain and apologize.

Don't feel too badly for blowing it this time. Hair grows back. It could have been a finger. "Cut and paste" time demands almost as much individual attention as a cardiac by-pass. Next time, get some help, or put Jack the Clipper at the opposite end of the table from anyone who sports more than a crew cut.

Sunday School Sue

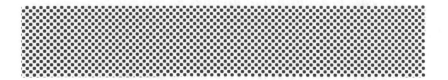

Some Things Infants And Toddlers Would Tell Their Teachers If They Could:

1. You may think you're baby sitting, but I think I'm in church.
2. I might be little, but I'm not deaf, so don't chit chat with the other nursery worker about things I shouldn't hear.
3. Please give me lots of room. I need to explore.
4. Please keep an eye on me constantly. I'm unaware of danger.
5. I don't know if it's the Sunday school hour or the church hour. Why does the quality of care sometimes change after that bell rings?
6. Please don't rush me. I need time to try out my ideas.
7. I wish you would get down on the floor and see what's at my eye level.
8. When I'm difficult to deal with, I'm probably tired or afraid.
9. I'm learning lessons and attitudes now that will stay with me the rest of my life.
10. The only way I can learn about God's love for me is through the love of God's people for me.

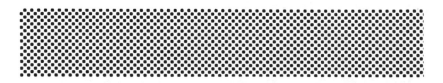

ALL ABOUT PRESCHOOLERS

Preschoolers are those little kids that think the church custodian lives in the broom closet and the preacher is God. They're the ones who believe the ushers get to keep the offering, and they think the sanctuary is the largest room in the world.

Preschoolers who go to Sunday school learn that God is love, and then they get pink lemonade and animal crackers. Preschoolers take fascinating field trips where they collect the wonders of nature like leaves, pinecones, rocks and beer cans.

Preschoolers are expensive to have around. If a Sunday school is on a limited budget, and a choice has to be made as to which department gets the furniture, space and equipment, be sure the best goes to the preschool department. The atmosphere that is created by the physical surroundings and the teacher are the only curriculum the church can provide for infants and toddlers. Preschoolers need plenty of room, as well as sturdy, safe, attractive and educationally valuable equipment and furnishings. All of that costs a lot of money.

Infants

The church best serves infants by providing safety, security, love, acceptance and dry diapers. When the church

provides for the needs of babies, the parents of those children naturally feel that the church is concerned for them and wants their participation in the life of the congregation.

Two-Year-Olds

Who hasn't heard of the "terrible two's"? Two-year-olds gained that reputation because they are developing their own personalities and independence, and that makes them seem somewhat negative at times. (Like when they scream NO! NO! NO! as they bite and kick you.) They are in perpetual motion, and they normally investigate, climb and get into trouble. It is usually more helpful to try to distract or protect them from what they don't need to be involved in rather than to try to discipline them. Both the memory and attention span of two-year-olds is very short.

In Sunday school two-year-olds need teachers who understand their developing autonomy and who have the patience and sense of humor to deal with it. They need adults who will keep them from harming themselves and others and who will provide acceptance that will enhance the child's self-image.

Three-Year-Olds

Terrible two's, thank the Lord, become trusting three's. Three-year-olds are actually eager to please, and they are interested in people other than themselves. They are becoming more cooperative, and they will frequently do what you tell them to do. However, they are usually tall enough and smart enough to open the classroom door and take off down the hall in search of Mommy and Daddy. They require constant supervision, which takes about one teacher for every four or five kids.

THREE-YEAR-OLDS NEED PLENTY OF SPACE

Like all preschoolers, three-year-olds need plenty of space. They should have opportunities to climb, jump, pull, explore and move around. In addition to active play, they need quiet times and lots of rest. They are fun to play with because they are highly imaginative, and they are beginning to share.

Four-Year-Olds

Four-year-olds are becoming more social, more independent, and more self-confident. Their motor coordination has improved, but they still can't do detailed work with their hands, and their attention span remains very short. Because of this, they will often tire of one activity and move on to another, leaving a task unfinished. About ten minutes is long enough for any group experience for four-year-olds. After that, they need a change of pace. They need to move about and be active. They are often talkative, imaginative and dramatic. Every other words is "why?"

FOUR-YEAR-OLDS
ARE MORE
SELF-CONFIDENT

Sunday school teachers need to provide opportunities for four-year-olds to experience individual and group play. Like children of all ages, four-year-olds need acceptance, love, freedom, protection and guidance.

Five-Year-Olds

A lot of people agree that kids are smarter than they used to be. That is probably true. There has been increased emphasis on early learning in recent years. Many five-year-olds have had a wide variety of experiences from a lifetime in daycare centers and preschools. Television has increased their vocabularies. The push for early learning just might give us a generation of five-year-olds who read Dostoevsky as they suck their thumbs and wet their pants.

No matter how much early learning they're exposed to, five-year-olds are still five-year-olds, and their most valuable work is play. Their attention span is lengthening, their vocabulary is growing and their motor coordination is improving, but they still need many of the same kinds of experiences that three and four-year-olds need.

Five-year-olds need plenty of freedom and flexibility in their schedules to allow for play and pretending. They are still active, noisy, curious, talkative and somewhat self-centered. Their self-confidence is improving as they learn a variety of skills like buttoning and unbuttoning their coats, pouring juice into a cup and tying their shoes.

A healthy balance of structure and freedom help give children in this age group the security and self-confidence they need. Limits should be set and enforced lovingly and kindly. Praise and appreciation for the child's accomplishments should be expressed freely and sincerely.

Sunday School Teachers For Preschoolers

Don't you believe it if someone says it's harder and more challenging to teach adults than young children. Teaching in the preschool department is not baby sitting. Those who teach preschoolers have a tremendous challenge and obligation, because children's attitudes about the church and their feelings about God are frequently set during these early years. You don't need a Ph.D. in early childhood development to teach Sunday school, but you should be willing to study and improve your understanding of the nature of children. Stick with it, and one of them might teach you to appreciate Dostoevsky.

TRY TO SPEAK AS CLEARLY AS POSSIBLE, OR...

Sunday School Sue

Dear Sunday School Sue,

Help! The weekday kindergarten is taking over my Sunday school room. When I arrive on Sunday mornings, I cannot find a thing. The tables and chairs have been rearranged, the books and toys are not where we left them and the bulletin board is covered with someone else's artwork. Whose room is it anyway? Some of those kids in weekday kindergarten are not even from families that belong to our church. I'm getting tired of the weekday kindergarten workers thinking they own the church building and equipment.

Sore in Springfield

Dear Sore,

You have a legitimate gripe, and usually weekday kindergarten staff people do too. As long as different groups share space and equipment, there will be a need for lots of communication and understanding.

Before you do anything else, think about it from the viewpoint of the weekday kindergarten. Those teachers are probably spending about 20 hours a week teaching in the room to your one hour. Through their program, they are touching the lives of children and their families who may have no other contact with the church. However, that does not give them the right to be inconsiderate about the property of the Sunday school.

Start by asking for a meeting of all teachers who use the room. At that meeting talk about the goals and purposes of the Sunday school and the weekday kindergarten. See how many common goals the two

programs share.

Talk about what the primary needs of each group are in terms of equipment, supplies and furnishings. Discuss what should be shared and what should not be shared. Try to be generous but practical. Keep an inventory of who owns what and who is responsible for replacement. Frequently the Sunday school can benefit from major equipment purchases by the weekday kindergarten, and vice versa.

While furniture, toys, puzzles, record players, books and teaching pictures can often be shared, it's not a good idea to share consumable supplies such as paper, paint, clay and glue.

Have a separate drawer, file cabinet, or supply closet for each group, complete with a lock. Locks are advisable, not because Sunday school and weekday kindergarten teachers can't be trusted to respect someone else's property, but because the church is frequently a very public place with scout troops, children's choirs and all sorts of folks in and out of rooms. Why should Sunday school teachers get mad at weekday kindergarten teachers for using all their modeling clay, when all the time it was those kids who were waiting while their mothers set tables for a circle luncheon.

Try to have two bulletin boards, one for each group. If that is not possible, maybe a two-sided one could be used. Or you could place hooks at the top of a bulletin board and have a second one overlay the first.

At your meeting, discuss how Sunday school teachers would like to find the room on Sunday morning and how weekday teachers would like for it to be on Monday morning. No one should have to arrive an hour before class time to find supplies and equipment or to rearrange furniture.

The weekday program probably has already made additional janitorial serv-

ices necessary. Even though teachers are not janitors, they have to assume some "housekeeping" responsibilities following their class sessions. It takes everyone working together to keep classrooms in apple pie order.

Communication, understanding and cooperation can lead to a workable and happy arrangement from which both the Sunday school and the weekday program can benefit.

By the way, one of the very first things you're supposed to learn at Sunday school is to share.

Sunday School Sue

OOEY-GOOEY FUN

Preschoolers love to feel modeling clay and finger paints ooze between their fingers. They need the experience of feeling and seeing how shapes and designs can be made with pliable materials. Here are some recipes for homemade clay and finger paints that are inexpensive and safe.

Finger Paints:

Place liquid starch in several baby food jars. Add food coloring. When you're through with finger painting for the day, screw the lids back on the jars and save for next time. Be sure kids wear paint smocks over Sunday clothes!

Modeling Clay:

3 cups flour
6 teaspoons cream of tartar
1 and 1/2 cups salt
3 cups water
3 tablespoons cooking oil

Mix all ingredients and cook until smooth. Food coloring may be added. Store in plastic bags in the refrigerator. It will harden if you leave it out.

Edible Clay:

1 cup peanut butter
3 tablespoons honey
enough powdered sugar to make it the right consistency

Edible clay provides a wonderful opportunity to teach that cleanliness is next to godliness. Have a lesson on the proper way to wash hands before you make edible clay. You can also use this experience to discuss what is edible and what is not.

Chapter 10:
IF WALLS COULD TALK
The Room Teaches

CLARA CLUTTER

C lara Clutter has the organizational ability of a tornado. The last time she threw anything away it was because someone convinced her that 1978 *TV Guides* had no value as collectors items and the exact schedules of television programs would not be repeated.

Clara has never closed a drawer or cabinet door in her life. That's mainly because it never occurred to her, but even if it did, the drawers and cabinets in her classroom are too stuffed to be closed.

CLARA CLUTTER

Some of her favorite statements are, "There's a lot of good left in that," — or "I might find a use for it someday," — or "You never know when you might need one of those."

The room where Clara teaches Sunday school makes the area behind most refrigerators look as antiseptic as an operating room. Neither Clara nor the church custodian can clean because of the accumulation of useless items that Clara can't get around to discarding.

The piano serves as a lost and found department as well as the repository for six years' worth of outdated curriculum materials. Its contents make the piano impossible to dust.

Window sills are homes for a number of dead house plants in pots that rest in disposable aluminum pie pans (she knew she'd find a use for those things). Windows so dirty they look frosted are partially covered by sagging draperies with about two-thirds of the hem out.

Chairs are mismatched, tables are wobbly-legged, and the

"I'M SURE IT'S AROUND HERE SoMEWHERE."

chalkboard hangs at a 45° angle. There are several flower vases scattered about the room, inside of which there is only a coating of dried green slime.

In Clara's class Christmas decorations are usually removed during Lent, and Easter pictures stay up until Thanksgiving. In the corner are several empty egg cartons and some red glitter left over from the craft project of a cub scout troop whose members long since graduated from high school.

Clara Clutter's motto is "I like to have everything within reach," so she never puts anything away. However, she never finds anything either. Her motto is, "I'm sure it's around here somewhere."

Rumor has it that an official from the health department came to check out Clara's classroom, but after one look he returned to his office, resigned his position and checked into a sanitarium for primal scream therapy.

HOW'S YOUR AMBIENCE?

The walls of a Sunday school room talk. A bright, tidy, cheerful room says, "Something good, pleasant and significant happens here." An unkept, unattractive classroom announces, "What goes on here is not important."

Furnishings, supplies and teaching equipment shout about the learning that takes place in a classroom. Furniture and surroundings appropriate for the age and activities of students give class members the message that they are expected, welcome and valuable. Inappropriate and inadequate teaching facilities say, "The people who come to Sunday school in this room don't matter very much to the one who's in charge of this space."

Ambience is a word that's been in vogue in recent years. It means *a surrounding or pervading atmosphere.* Sunday school teachers need to be careful about the ambience they create, because students are extremely sensitive to it, whether they realize it or not. Ambience includes more than physical surroundings, but physical surroundings are a vital part of ambience.

The ambience starts before people enter the room. Kids aren't too keen on walking down long dark halls or up or down steep stairs to arrive at a tacky, shabby room. It helps if the approach to the classroom is well lighted, inviting and attractive.

Because people learn through all five senses, the atmosphere created for the teaching-learning experience determines how receptive learners are. The room teaches. The walls talk. The message comes across — loud and clear.

Make Friends With The Janitor

"Oh," some would protest, "I'm not the janitor." Of course not. And the janitor is not the teacher either. A clean, pleasant inviting room takes both janitor and teacher working together. Janitors are afraid to throw away anything, and who could blame them. They probably got jumped on once for throwing out some string and an empty coffee can that someone was saving for a craft project. Teachers must assume responsibility for getting trash into the wastebasket. Janitors usually take it from there.

Chances are that if teachers give the impression they aren't concerned about the appearance of the room, the janitor won't be concerned either.

It's very likely that the paths of Sunday school teachers

DON'T WAIT FOR A COMPLAINT FROM THE E.P.A.

and janitors don't cross during the week. It's also likely that the janitor receives multiple and sometimes conflicting instructions from a number of different people. Teachers should learn the expected procedures and proper channels of communication for the janitor. To get a message to the janitor might take a call to the church office, or it might be possible to leave a note. Lucky teachers will be able to become friends with the janitor and work as a team to have a clean, attractive classroom.

Sunday School Sue

Dear Sunday School Sue,

We have a problem in our preschool department. So many people have donated second-hand toys, games and books to the Sunday school, that our classroom looks like a yard sale. I teach among mountains of dirty stuffed animals, limbless dolls, torn books and puzzles without all their pieces.

I hesitate to take the bull by the horns and dispose of this trash because it does not belong to me. I don't want to hurt the feelings of people who gave the toys to the church. What is the proper procedure for dealing with this situation?

Overwhelmed in Omaha

Dear Overwhelmed,

Don't hesitate. Take the bull by the horns. There are two ways to do it. First, you could boldly back a truck up to the church door and haul off everything in question. Take it to Goodwill or the garbage dump. Or you could disguise yourself as a bag lady and carry it off a bagfull at a time.

However you decide to accomplish the deed, get it done. There is a helpful rule of thumb in deciding what to keep: WHEN IN DOUBT, THROW IT OUT.

Ask the appropriate committee in your church to request that people who want to make donations to the preschool division do so in the form of cash or checks. The preschool coordinator or teachers should then purchase new toys, which they have thoughtfully and carefully selected.

If money is not available to purchase new toys immediately, see if you can borrow two or three sturdy toys to be used for one Sunday only. Be sure the borrowed items are returned promptly and in good condition. The next Sunday, borrow something else. Meanwhile, ask for assistance from the church to purchase needed equipment. Toys are the teaching equipment of preschoolers. Cluttering up the classroom with castoffs does not teach the lesson that should be taught to preschoolers or their parents.

Sunday School Sue

CLEAN UP, PAINT UP, FIX UP

Phyllis Diller is living proof that it pays to fix up. It will be cheaper and less painful to give your Sunday school room a facelift than it was for Ms. Diller to make her improvements, and the results can be equally dramatic.

A gallon of paint will cover a multitude of sins. Painting forces you to clean up before and after, and it usually leads to additional improvements.

If you are in a church that can afford to hire professional painters to come in and re-do the building, you can use that occasion as impetus to do some things to the room that hired workmen cannot do. If your church wants volunteer help in refurbishing, you have a challenge and an opportunity to excel.

Whatever you do, go through the proper channels. Check with the minister, trustees or whoever has responsibility for physical improvements to the building before doing anything. Make sure permission is granted and plans are approved before you begin to enlist volunteer helpers to spruce up your Sunday school room.

Consider a painting party. Consider it carefully. There are definite advantages and disadvantages.

Advantages Of A Painting Party

There's nothing that improves camaraderie among class members like a good project that requires physical labor and cooperation. If you want to improve the "group feeling," enjoy fellowship on a level different from that of Sunday morning, and provide a great opportunity for class members to become better acquainted, you can do it with a painting party.

Painting the classroom will give people a feeling of pride and accomplishment in their work. It can also give them an opportunity to serve their church. It instills a sense of responsibility for the room and a feeling of belonging there.

The do-it-ourselves approach is a cheap way to get the room painted. Professional painters are expensive.

Disadvantages Of A Painting Party

With volunteer workers, you might not get the neat, professional looking paint job you'd have if you pay a crew to do it for you. This is especially true if you have a group of teenagers who want to paint their classroom. In most cases, teenagers will get more paint on each other than on the walls.

Another thing to consider is that Sunday school classes don't own the rooms where they meet. Once they have painted and redecorated the room, people feel that it is theirs. Sometimes it is necessary for classroom space to be reshuffled to accommodate changing needs within the congregation. Be sure that everyone knows that even if members paint the classroom, that does not give them a deed to the property.

How To Organize A Painting Party

If yours is a children's class, invite all parents to a meeting to discuss the idea. If parents agree to tackle the project, get a parent who does not care to paint to serve as baby sitter during the painting party. If you're dealing with an adult class, involve as many people as possible, even if you have to work in shifts.

After permission has been granted, plans approved and volunteers enlisted, decide on a time convenient to the majority of the group. Don't plan to find a time that suits everyone.

NO TIME IS FULLY SATISFACTORY FOR EVERYONE

There's no such thing.

Allow more than one evening to accomplish the job. It will probably take one evening or Saturday for advance cleaning and preparation.

Make a written list of needed tools and equipment: Paint, paint remover, brushes, rollers, paint pads, dropcloths, sandpaper, pans, rags, etc. Pass the list around and ask people to sign up for what they can furnish. Those who have no painting equipment at home might want to make a donation to purchase it. With labor furnished, perhaps the paint can be purchased with church funds.

Select a supervisor. Someone experienced with a paint brush needs to delegate responsibilities, answer questions and keep things moving. This must be done tactfully and fairly. There's no point in offending anyone over a Sunday school project.

Those who prefer not to paint, but who would like to help in some way could provide refreshments for break time if it's an evening party. If it's an all day event, they could be in charge of lunch.

Make sure that cleanup responsibilities are assigned ahead of time. When cleanup time rolls around, the fun and glamour have worn off, and folks have a tendency to poop out on you.

Once the room is painted and redecorated, have an open house. Invite the congregation to drop by after church and share in the joy of the shipshape classroom. Then just watch as spirits and attendance soar.

Special Touches For The Youth Department

In addition to a bright tidy room with sufficient tables and chairs, teenagers need a place they can call their own. If possible, let them select the colors and decorative scheme (within reason). School pennants or banners made by the young people can lend a personal touch.

Teenagers might want to furnish their room with donated pieces of upholstered furniture. This is usually a dreadful mistake. They'll end up with dirty, shabby castoff rocker-recliners and sofas that take up space, look terrible, aren't comfortable and are certainly not conducive to learning. Take all such furniture to Goodwill.

Get a bulletin board just for clippings and pictures about accomplishments of students. Awards in athletics, cheerleading, drama, debate, science fair, music or whatever should be recognized. Encourage students to bring these clippings, as it's possible that the teacher will miss some. Try to make sure that no one is overlooked.

Let the teenagers select a convenient Saturday for cleanup day. After cleanup time, they can decorate the room and have lunch. They'll probably have fun and you can bet your last peso that they'll do more work than mom can get them to do at home.

It's important that they feel any project is their own. If they think adults are trying to impose work on them, they'll have the enthusiasm of a tree stump. If it's their idea and they can plan some of the details, it becomes an adventure.

A Children's Classroom Party

Children of elementary age will probably be eager to help spruce up their Sunday school room. It might be easier for the teacher to do the work alone, but the value is more in the participation of the class members than in the cleanliness of the room.

Have a "Room Party." Invite children to bring an inexpensive gift for the room. It could be chalk, thumbtacks, a small plant, a stained glass window ornament, a pretty magazine picture for the bulletin board, or whatever the kids want to bring.

Make a game out of chores by writing descriptions of jobs to be done on slips of paper. Let the children draw a piece of paper from a hat. Watch the giggles, moans, groans and surprised faces when they read their task. Make sure that tasks are described in great detail. Instructions must be explicit.

Some jobs elementary children can handle nicely are washing the chalkboard, dusting, emptying trash, straightening books, removing things from the bulletin board, watering plants, sorting crayons, running a vacuum cleaner, filing story pictures and sweeping. All elementary age children are major league champions at emptying the pencil sharpener.

After about 30 minutes of work, reward the kids with refreshments and a game or two. You and the janitor could do the tasks more quickly and thoroughly than the kids, but that's not the point. They need to take pride in their room and feel that they have contributed to it.

A Preschool Toy Shower

Why not invite preschoolers and their parents to a toy shower? Distribute a "want list" ahead of time so parents will have an idea of what is needed in the classroom. Be sure that items on the list are reasonably priced and available. Two or three parents could go in together to purchase more expensive toys.

Ask that toys be gift-wrapped. When children arrive, refreshments can be served, and then each child can open the gift brought by another child. (Draw names or numbers.)

Allow the children to play with the toys, but make sure they understand that the gift is for the room, and it must be left in the room so it will be there to play with next Sunday.

While children play with the toys, take advantage of the time to get to know parents and discuss with them the aims and goals of the pre-school department. Keep your eyes and ears open, and you'll probably learn a lot from the parents that will help you understand and deal with the children.

Try A Nursery Shower

Everybody loves to see pretty baby shower gifts. Invite

parents of infants to attend a nursery shower. Ask them to bring a gift that will be used to help care for their baby in the church nursery. Useful items such as disposable diapers, crib sheets, blankets, pre-moistened towellettes, crib pads and tissues might be suggested. Decorative wall plaques, mobiles, a new trash can, new curtains and infant's toys are also possibilities.

It would be easier for the nursery worker to get a check from the church office and go to the supermarket and buy these items. But getting the parents involved gives them a sense of belonging and lets them know that the nursery workers are concerned about their infants. The party is an ideal time to get better acquainted and discuss any problems or needs there are in the nursery.

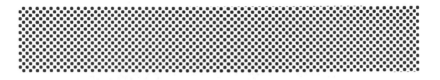

What Every Sunday School Room Should Have:

1. **A teacher**
2. **Some students**
3. **Adequate lighting**
4. **Good ventilation**
5. **Comfortable temperature**
6. **A periodic cleaning**
7. **Order**
8. **Organization**
9. **Furniture suitable to the age and size of class members**
10. **A sign outside the door announcing who meets there**

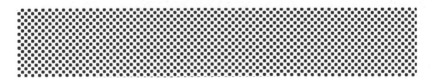

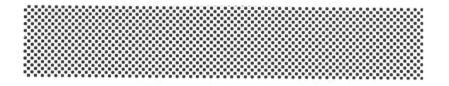

What Every Sunday School Room Should Not Have:

1. Lead paint peeling off the walls
2. Asbestos flaking from the ceiling
3. Dirt
4. Clutter (old literature, leftover craft supplies, etc.)
5. Marijuana growing in the window sill
6. Disorder
7. Radioactive fallout
8. Dead plants
9. Castoff, mismatched, ill-suited furniture
10. Rats and roaches

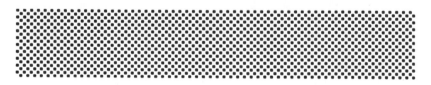

WHERE TO ORDER FURNITURE, EQUIPMENT AND SUPPLIES

There are many places to buy good furniture, equipment and supplies for your Sunday school classroom. Most denominations have bookstores that special order furnishings for you if they don't stock what you need. The following places will send you attractive catalogs that will make you wish you could throw out everything in your classroom and start over. This is by no means an exhaustive list, but it will get you started.

Cokesbury Service Center
1661 N. Northwest Highway
Park Ridge, IL 60068
(312)299-4411

Cokesbury Service Center
1635 Adrian Road
Burlingame, CA 94014
(415)692-3562

Cokesbury Service Center
201 Eighth Avenue South
Nashville, TN 37202
(615)749-6113

Baptist Bookstore
2930 Flowers Rd., So.
Atlanta, GA 30341
(404)458-8131

Presbyterian Bookstore
341 Ponce de Leon Ave., NE
Atlanta, GA 30365
(404)873-1549

Baptist Bookstore
4316 Brainerd Rd.
Chattanooga, TN 37411
(615)629-2593

IT'S NOT WHAT YOU HAVE BUT WHAT YOU DO WITH IT

In the land of perfection, all Sunday school rooms are spacious, attractive and clean. There is plenty of light, the temperature is always comfortable and ventilation is good. In these perfect rooms, furniture is not scratched, paint does not peel and rugs are never stained or threadbare. Shelves, cabinets and other storage space are adequate and well organized. Furniture is comfortable, and there are never any splinters on the chairs to pull runs in teachers' pantyhose.

The rooms are soundproof, and there are room-darkening shades to be used with the classes' very own film and filmstrip projectors and VCR. The perfectly tuned piano has all its teeth.

Classrooms in this utopia have plenty of maps and a good bulletin board with a never-ending supply of thumbtacks. Beside the large chalkboard there is a perpetually blooming chalk tree.

In adult classrooms, there is a coffee counter with hot water constantly available so people can make a cup of instant anything at any time.

In children's classrooms, tables and chairs fit the size of the students. There is a long counter with built-in sink at the children's level. Picture files are in perfect order, and craft and art supplies are neatly arranged in the craft closet.

Preschool rooms are bright, cheerful and squeaky clean. Play equipment is safe, sturdy and appropriate for the age and abilities of the children. Each classroom has a private restroom with fixtures low enough for little ones.

The large nursery is immaculate but at the same time warm and inviting. Colors are soft, pleasant and relaxing. There are more than enough cribs and rocking chairs, plenty

"CLEANLINESS IS INDEED NEXT TO GODLINESS."
— JOHN WESLEY

of changing tables and an adjacent restroom.

Ah perfection! Wouldn't it be lovely!

Let's face it — most Sunday school teachers will never work in perfect physical facilities. Many teach in crowded, unattractive spaces that are poorly arranged and have whatever furniture can be scraped together. Countless Sunday school classes are held in basement rooms with pipes overhead and no electrical outlets, much less a VCR to plug in. Some teach in one-room churches where several classes are in progress simultaneously, and their space is the back pew on the left. Ventilation for some is a cardboard fan from the local funeral home, and equipment is a half dead piano.

Although perfectly furnished rooms are desirable, they are not an absolute necessity for learning, so if you're stuck in a crummy room, do what you can to perk it up, think of Abraham Lincoln and keep plugging away.

Inadequate, unattractive and ill-equipped classrooms give teachers an opportunity to use their creativity. You know the old saying about making lemonade when you're handed a lemon.

If you teach in the basement and the pipes are exposed, use them creatively by hanging wires from them for mobiles, posters or pictures.

If you share a fellowship hall with other classes, see if someone can make portable partitions that can be used as bulletin boards as well as sound and vision barriers. In some cases, styrofoam panels could be suspended from the ceiling to form room dividers. Fabric curtains have been used for years to make temporary dividers. They absorb sound, and pictures can be pinned on them. Large rolling chalkboards and bulletin boards can serve double duty as room dividers.

In crowded rooms, move out unnecessary furniture. It's amazing what can become unnecessary in a pinch. Sometimes in crowded children's classes, chairs are in the way. Children like to stand to work at tables, and they enjoy sitting on the floor on an area rug. Without chairs to bump around, the room will be quieter, and fewer people will be kicked.

Where there is no bulletin board, tape things on the walls with masking tape. Seldom used doors make fine bulletin boards. In the absence of a chalkboard, write on newsprint or butcher paper with a felt-tip marker. Need another shelf or display area.? Try the window sill.

What about the perennial storage problem? The secret is organization. A large cardboard box can be used to file pictures and hold teaching and craft supplies.

Get rid of droopy, faded curtains. Sparkling clean windows make the room look larger and brighter, so if your room is small and dark, keep the windows bare. If you must have a window treatment, consider a simple ruffle or valance across the top.

Look at the light fixture. It's possible that changing it could make the entire room look new. There are inexpensive fluorescent fixtures that are easy to install and energy efficient.

Do the best you can with what you have to work with. Physical surroundings are important in the teaching-learning situation. However, the most important ingredients are the teacher, the learners and the relationship between the two. Think of all the presidents, statesmen and great educators who are products of the one-room schoolhouse. Think of all the ministers, missionaries and people of God who came to know the Lord in a one-room church's Sunday school.

WHAT IT'S NICE TO HAVE IN SUNDAY SCHOOL ROOMS

One of the first things you learned in Sunday school was to share. Sunday schools everywhere continue to provide the opportunity to put that noble action into practice. You probably get to share audio-visual equipment — films, filmstrips, projectors, screens, VCR's, record players, records. Perhaps you share maps , pictures, hand puppets, flannelboards and other teaching supplies and equipment. When extra large crowds are at church for special events, you probably share chairs and tables.

You also share space. Uninformed adults have been known to feel that because children are smaller than grown-ups, the little ones need smaller classrooms. Not so. Kids need to move around, and they need space for play and learning activities. In the land of perfection, young children's classrooms have 35 square feet of space per child. Adults usually sit still at Sunday school, so it's possible to put them in smaller rooms.

Every Sunday school room cannot be perfectly furnished and equipped, but here are some things it would be nice for rooms to have, in addition to Bibles and curriculum materials.

Youth And Adult Classrooms

Tables to sit around
Chairs
Bulletin board
Chalkboard
Shelf space
Storage space in cabinets or closets
A set of teaching maps
Piano
Audio visual equipment
Pencils, paper

Children's Classrooms

Child-size chairs and tables
Bulletin board
Chalkboard
Book shelves with appropriate books
Audio visual equipment
Appropriate pictures with picture file
Storage cabinets or closets
Flannelboard
Glue
Tape
Crayons

LEARN TO SHARE

Felt tip markers
Newsprint
Construction paper
Pencils
Pencil sharpener
Scissors
Stapler and staples
Holepunch
Computer

Preschool Classrooms

Chairs (9-12 inches high)
Tables (16-22 inches high)
Low chalkboard
Low bulletin board
Book table with appropriate books
Nature table or interest center
Worship center table (for open Bible, offering plate, etc.)
Low shelves
Set of large wooden blocks
Wooden cars, trucks and trains
Set of wooden "family" figures
Safe, sturdy toys (no small pieces or sharp edges)
Audio-visual equipment
Easel with washable paints
Newsprint or butcher paper
Smocks (adult shirts buttoned in back)
Climbing equipment
Rocking boat that doubles as steps
Doll bed, dolls, dollclothes
Telephone (you needn't choose any telephone company)
Dress-up clothes and hats
Wall mirror
Wooden child-size stove, sink, refrigerator, kitchen table
Unbreakable toy dishes and cooking utensils
Rhythm band instruments
Modeling clay
Construction paper
Crayons
Blunt scissors
Glue
Storage cabinets or closets

Infant Nursery

Sturdy cribs (three feet of space between each one)
Zippered covers on crib mattresses
Enough crib sheets to have a clean one for each baby
Mattress pads
Playpens
Swing
Reclining infant seat
Changing table
Rocking chairs for adult workers
Storage for each infant's belongings
Disposable diapers
Pre-moistened towellettes
Tissues
Paper towels
Storage cabinets or closets

If this list makes you feel that your teaching facilities are inadequate, you are not alone. You have something to work toward.

Chapter 11:
MY, HOW YOU'VE GROWN

WHAT MAKES SUNDAY SCHOOLS GROW?

Desire And Organization

One of the main ingredients necessary for Sunday school growth is the desire to grow. But simply wanting something is seldom enough. You have to make things happen, or at least help them along. (Sometimes you have to get out of the way and let the Lord move in his own mysterious way!)

Organization includes setting goals, identifying prospects

and analyzing present attendance and class structure. A good honest, objective look at ourselves, while sometimes difficult, is necessary if growth is to take place. Pretend you're a visitor in your church's Sunday school. If you knew nothing about how things got to be the way they are, or all the reasons they are that way, how would you see the Sunday school? How would you feel if you visited? Would you be eager to return?

Content And Teaching

A growing Sunday school must be based on sound theological and educational principles in keeping with the doctrines of your church. If the printed curriculum used is provided by the publishing house that serves your denomination, you're on safe ground to assume the material is in keeping with theological and educational standards acceptable to your church.

When in doubt about content, curriculum or teaching methods, check with your minister. He or she should be your strongest ally in working toward a growing Sunday school. Without support of the pastor, you're probably on a sinking ship anyway.

Growing Sunday schools have teachers that are recruited honestly. Don't believe it if someone says "There's nothing to

WHEN IN DOUBT CHECK WITH YOUR MINISTER

teaching that class." Prospective teachers need to know what's in store for them when they take a class. They should be told exactly what is expected of them — how long they are to teach, what will be provided in the way of equipment and literature and who will substitute when necessary.

Growing Sunday schools also have well trained teachers. The minister should be able to direct teachers to sources of training within the denomination such as workshops, institutes, lab schools and seminars. Church's should make every effort to pay expenses of teachers who are willing to attend these educational events. It's a better investment than blue chip stocks.

Flexibility

If you want to guarantee that your Sunday school will *not* grow, be sure to insist on doing things as you've always done them. On the other hand, if you want to get ready for significant growth, start by taking a fresh look at your traditional programs and structures. Are they meeting with declining success year in and year out? If so, why continue with them? Be willing to rearrange schedules, classroom arrangements and traditional ways of doing things.

Carefully study the classroom space available to see if it is being used in the most efficient way possible. A Sunday school class might believe it owns the room where it meets, but it doesn't. Willingness to adapt and change is a key ingredient in Sunday school growth.

Grouping

Small groups grow better than large groups. New groups grow better than long established groups. It's a fact of life. Studies have shown that in groups where it's possible to have eye to eye contact among group members, a healthy atmosphere of caring and growth can be established. The creation of new classes will afford more growth than efforts to bring people into existing classes.

Groups grow when members feel the support, love, care, and concern of one another. This is easier to accomplish in a smaller group than in a larger one.

Groups grow when they enjoy occasional social experiences together. Times of fellowship such as class parties and trips enable group members to get to know each other better, and a genuine concern for one another is a natural outgrowth.

Celebration

In a growing Sunday school, there will be plenty of praise to go around for everyone. Set aside times to honor teachers and leaders with services of consecration and dedication as well as teacher appreciation banquets or programs. Show appreciation for all those who attend Sunday school as well. Talk about growth and improvements so that people will be aware of how well things are going. Look for the good. Affirm the good. Show appreciation for the positive accomplishments of groups and individuals.

Don't be afraid to face up to those elements of the Sunday school that are not so good. Constantly evaluate, not in order to criticize, but in order to improve. Needs will change from time to time. Be ready to change when necessary. Don't be surprised if you experience a few growing pains. But don't worry about them. They don't last long, and the rewards are worth them.

WHAT BRINGS PEOPLE BACK?

Former Sunday school and church dropouts who are active once again identified their reasons for returning as follows:

35% — Need for Christian Fellowship

21% — Move to new community or coming of new pastor

17% — Desire for children to be in Sunday school

17% — New religious experience

10% — Someone invited them; they felt needed and wanted.*

---

*Statistics from "What Brings People Back" by Warren Hartman, Board of Discipleship, from the PEOPLE TO PEOPLE tabloid, page 1, Summer 1985. Copyright 1985 by Graded Press. Used by permission.

Best Yet Excuses For Not Attending Sunday School:

1. While I'm at Sunday school, John Baresfoot Tipton might come to my house with a cashier's check for one million dollars.
2. If I go to Sunday school, I might miss the Jehovah's Witnesses and not get my copy of *Watchtower*.
3. I might step on a rattlesnake walking from the church parking lot to the Sunday school classroom.
4. Libyan terrorists might have planted a bomb in the Sunday school classroom.
5. I might run into some hypocrites.
6. I might be exposed to something communicable.
7. I might catch poison ivy from the potted plant on the window sill in the Sunday school classroom.
8. I'd have to wear shoes and a shirt.
9. I'll miss re-runs of *Mister Rogers' Neighborhood*.
10. If I stay home and dig a hole in my backyard, I might strike oil.

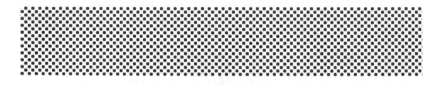

Most Overused Excuses For Not Attending Sunday School:

1. Sunday is my only day to sleep late.
2. I don't have a thing to wear.
3. It's all I can do to get to the 11 o'clock worship service.
4. I might be called on to pray.
5. I might be called on to answer a question.
6. I might be called on to read the Bible.
7. Sunday school is full of hypocrites.
8. I went once, and people were not friendly.
9. We just bought lakefront property and a boat.
10. I used to go, but I got out of the habit.

Sunday School Sue

Dear Sunday School Sue:

I'm afraid our Sunday school class is dying. We started out as an active young adult class about 10 years ago. Attendance has varied, but frequently in years past we have had as many as 30 present. Now we average less than 10 each Sunday. Originally our teacher was the associate minister, but he moved to another church a couple of years ago. Now we post a calendar on the bulletin board in the classroom, and each class member signs up for a Sunday to be responsible for the lesson. Those who don't wish to teach the class themselves are free to find another teacher or speaker to come in and "do the lesson." We cover a variety of topics, and we use whatever literature or Bible study helps the teacher for the day selects.

We used to have interesting, inspiring lessons and great Sunday school parties. Lately, it seems no one really cares much about the class. Everyone is too busy to get actively involved. What can we do to stimulate interest and participation?

Puzzled in Peoria

Dear Puzzled,

My research indicates that rotation works well for car pools and the earth, but it is totally inappropriate for marriage partners and Sunday school teachers.

If you want your class to be revitalized, you need to do five things:

1. FIND A TEACHER — Get your minister, education committee, or whoever is in charge of such things in your church to help the class recruit a lively, interesting,

intelligent, and dedicated teacher who will show up every Sunday and lead the class in a meaningful study.

2. FIND A BOOK — A commmittee from within the class should work with the minister or other qualified staff member to select a Bible study book or other curriculum resource that the class can use for at least three months. Then select another one.

3. FIND A PROJECT — Get the group to select a service project that requires working together to accomplish a significant goal. Try to come up with a project that demands physical activity on the part of class members. Make sure it's more physical than writing a check.

4. FIND A CARE COMMITTEE — This could be composed of officers, but if your officers are not too swift, find somebody else. The CARE COMMITTEE should send cards, make phone calls, and visit absentees and prospective members.

5. BURN THAT CALENDAR — And never rotate "teachers" again!

Go get 'em!

Sunday School Sue

DIVIDE AND CONQUER

If you think dividing a Sunday school class will cause it to dwindle away, you're wrong. Dividing a class can promote growth and vitality, *provided* the surgery is performed with skill, care and sensitivity.

Buy why would anyone want to divide a class? There are two very good reasons:

1. The class has grown too much.

2. The class has not grown enough.

The *Pairs and Spares Class* is a good example of the first problem. (By the way, don't hold that silly name against them — people all over the country have thought it was cute.) The class was formed six years ago as a Bible study group

198

"YOU LOOK FAMILIAR."

EVEN A DIVIDED WORM CAN GROW ANOTHER HEAD.

composed of seven young married couples and three singles. With 17 people on roll, the class had an average attendance of about a dozen. This worked well for several years. Twelve was a good number for discussions, and most class members had homes large enough to accommodate the class Christmas party and summer cookout held each year.

For a number of reasons, (good Bible study literature, a well prepared and interesting teacher and friendly, concerned members) the class began to grow by leaps and bounds. There were 40 on roll, and average attendance was 28.

The growth was good news and bad news. Anyone who can do eighth grade math can quickly determine that 12 out of 17 is a better attendance percentage than 28 out of 40. But 28 people made a room full, so the class seemed to be doing great. No one worried much about the dozen absentees, because there was always a good crowd at Sunday school. Anyway, if all 40 had shown up at one time, there wouldn't have been enough chairs.

The summer cookout continued to work well, because 40 people don't fill up a back yard. (Those absent from Sunday school managed to make the party every time.) However, people stopped volunteering their homes for the Christmas party, not only because no one had seating capacity for the crowd, but no one had kitchen counter space sufficient to accommodate all the covered dishes. One year the class Christmas party was held in the church fellowship hall, and one year they tried the community center, but in both places, that special warm, festive atmosphere found in a home during the Christmas season was missing.

The class reached a plateau. Attendance leveled off, and group discussion became dominated by the same few people who were extroverted enough not to be intimidated by expressing an opinion or venturing an answer in a large gathering. That special closeness and fellowship that had once characterized the class slipped badly.

The *Pairs and Spares Class* elected to have major surgery. However, the members were not content to divide the class completely, cutting all ties with those who would end up in another class, and losing contact with the teacher. And as always, there was a shortage of well qualified, willing teachers. This is how they solved their problem.

The class moved to the fellowship hall. They were carefully and thoughtfully divided into four groups of ten each, with each person's attendance regularity, talkativeness and personality taken into account. Each group sat around one of the large tables in the fellowship hall. Each group selected a secretary who was willing to keep up with attendance and oversee the group's membership drive. A friendly competition was encouraged to see which group could have the best attendance record.

The teacher recruited a leader from each group, and the four leaders worked under the direction of the teacher. Every week these five people either met or talked on the phone after they had studied the lesson. The teacher told the group leaders how the lesson would be approached and gave them a list of discussion questions related to the lesson. Frequently the four group leaders had valuable ideas that had not occurred to the teacher. The sharing was stimulating for everyone involved.

On Sunday morning, the class had coffee and fellowship 15 minutes before class time. When it was time to start, they sat at their appointed tables as the teacher spoke to the entire class, introducing the lesson and suggesting topics for discussion or questions to answer within the groups at the tables. Fifteen to 20 minutes of class time was designated for discussions within the small "table" groups.

About ten minutes before the bell, the teacher called on each group leader to report the most important findings, decisions or insights of the groups. Sometimes there were unanswered questions directed at the teacher or other group leaders or members. The teacher summarized the main points of the lesson and tied together any loose ends before reminding the class of the material to be covered in next week's lesson.

People who were absent were truly missed by the others at their table, and absentees were called during the week and checked on. In time, this closeness and concern for group members, and the friendly competition for the attendance award resulted in significant growth, so that five groups were necessary, and then six.

Also in time, the individual group leaders became so confident in their leadership abilities that they were willing to assume full responsibility for teaching a class.

Before most folks knew it, the church had built additional classrooms, and the groups chose to become full-fledged classes with their very own room, teacher, Christmas party and summer cookout.

However, each class did so well that in a few years, they had to draw straws to see which ones got to use the fellowship hall in order to divide into four groups and sit around tables to discuss the topics suggested by the teacher.

IT WORKS BOTH WAYS

The *Happy Workers Class* used the same technique to solve a different problem. This group had met for a number of years as a lecture class with the same faithful teacher, expounding Sunday after Sunday on ideas that class members had heard dozens of times. (Some of the regular attenders could finish the teacher's sentences.) The service projects of the *Happy Workers* grew fewer and farther apart as enthusiasm first leveled off and finally evaporated. At the classes' high point there were over 50 on roll. Participation deteriorated, and average attendance was less than 20.

By dividing into two groups of ten each and working on individual participation, discussion, attendance rewards, and innovative teaching methods, the *Happy Workers* gradually became three, then four, and then five groups of ten each.

In time, they too had a problem with who got the fellowship hall, and where all the classes would meet. Fortunately, it became fashionable for churches to build fancy new Family Life Centers, that included additional classroom facilities, and all the classes that were spin-offs from the *Happy Workers* found rooms in which they could meet.

HOW TO MAKE IT WORK

Just as the surgeon does not attempt brain surgery without proper preparation, equipment, skill and willingness to work, so a Sunday school class should not be divided without

YOU
NEED A TRUE
DIPLOMAT TO
EXPLAIN YOUR
PROPOSED CHANGE.

all of the above. Here's what you need:

1. A diplomatic person to explain the plan to the class and convince them of its benefits so that they want to make the change. If the class feels the plan is imposed on them against their wills, it will fail for sure.

2. A well qualified teacher who is willing to study the lesson at the first of the week and spend some time with the group leaders by the middle of the week.

3. Group leaders who will cooperate with the teacher and learn to be effective discussion directors.

4. Group secretaries who will faithfully record attendance, send cards to absentees, and call group members to keep in touch.

5. People who will take turns arriving early to prepare coffee and stay late to clean up the mess.

6. Study books and teachers guides that lend themselves

to discussion-type teaching.

7. A room large enough to accommodate everyone involved.

8. Sufficient tables and chairs.

9. A committee (perhaps the teacher, secretaries, and leaders) who know class members well enough to divide the class into workable and effective groups.

10. Plenty of patience. It won't work overnight.

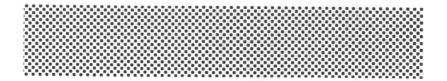

Good Reasons To Go To Sunday School:

1. Believe it or not, there are still some things you could learn about the Bible, the Christian faith, and the meaning of life.
2. The best people in town are there.
3. You won't be home when the door-to-door evangelists call.
4. There's little on TV at that time except preaching that's probably inferior to teaching you could hear at Sunday school.
5. In today's complex world, you need all the help you can get to walk the straight and narrow.
6. Your church needs you to help support its programs and influence others to take advantage of them.
7. You'll find a Christian support group to help you through life's difficult moments.
8. You'll find an opportunity for personal ministry through the service projects of the class.
9. You won't be late for the 11 o'clock worship service.
10. The devil might get you if you don't go.

"YOU'RE THE ONLY KID IN THE SUNDAY SCHOOL WITH A 50-YEAR ATTENDANCE PIN."

LIFESPAN OF A SUNDAY SCHOOL CLASS

Almost all churches have at least one Sunday school class composed of dedicated saints who have been attending faithfully for the past 50 years. Probably the class has a fine history of Bible study and service to the church and community. The group rightly deserves the respect, love and admiration of all.

In recent years the average attendance of the class has more than likely declined markedly. Members have gone on to their rewards or for reasons of age and health are no longer able to attend. What do you do with a group like this that is dwindling away to nothing? How does the class get more members and inject new blood into itself?

Let's face it. Unlike the kids of *Fame*, Sunday school classes do not live forever. It is normal for classes to live out their lifespans and die. Sunday school classes have periods of birth, greatest growth, waning and finally death. Sometimes the dying process takes many years; sometimes it happens more quickly. This is a threatening concept and will not be easily accepted, but it is a fact of life.

If a sick class can be helped by getting a new teacher, different literature, better facilities or whatever, by all means, it should be helped to revitalize itself. But there are times when the only merciful thing to do is to let a class live out its lifespan in quietness and dignity.

Sunday school classes are like people, not mules. If your mule breaks a leg, you shoot him. Not so with your Aunt Ethyl — or with Sunday school classes. However, there is one similarity between mules and Sunday school classes. (Okay, maybe there's more than one, but we're just going to talk about one!) When your mule is too far gone — for whatever reason — you get another mule. When a Sunday school class is on the wane, you *start another class* — not for members of the waning class, but for those not presently in any Sunday school class.

Statistics show that a new person within the congregation is much more likely to attend a newly formed group than one where the members have formed close bonds by being together for years. It's not that the long established classes don't welcome newcomers, it's just that a new person does not usually find it easy to be a part of a group that has a long history in which he does not share.

But how do you make funeral arrangements for a Sunday school class? It depends on the individual situation, but often the kindest thing to do when a group has dwindled beyond survival on its own, is to combine it with a younger, more active class. More than likely there will be strong feelings among class members concerning the solution to the problem. Those wishes should be honored as much as possible. Death is seldom easy, even for Sunday school classes.

HOW TO START A NEW SUNDAY SCHOOL CLASS

To start a new Sunday school class, you must mind your P's and Q's. There are a dozen of them — ten P's and two Q's.

Planning:

Things don't get done by accident — at least not when it comes to starting a new Sunday school class. Organizing a new group that will sustain itself successfully takes hard work and careful planning by a number of people.

Start with a committee that sees the need for a new class. Some of the committee members will no doubt become members of the new class, and their enthusiasm will be contagious.

Prospects:

The first thing the committee will do is discover who might be in the new class. Go through the church roll with a fine tooth comb, comparing the list with Sunday school enrollment. You will probably come up with a lot of names of adults who are not in any Sunday school class.

Another way to get a good prospect list is to put a questionnaire in the Sunday bulletin or the church's mid-week newsletter surveying the congregation. The survey could help determine names of prospective class members as well as topics that people would like to study.

In some situations, it would be advisable to start a class only for "newcomers." Many churches are large enough to have a "singles" class. Others might need a "young adult" class. However, most adults are capable of relating to adults of other ages and stations in life, and it is usually more interesting not to limit a class to a certain age group or marital status.

Frequently a group can be successfully formed on the basis of a common interest in a particular subject, such as Bible study, a social or ethical issue, church history, or whatever.

When you find at least six interested prospects, you have enough people to start a new class.

Place:

In growing churches it is sometimes difficult to find a spare classroom to house a newly formed group. If an empty room is not available, try the choir loft, pastor's study, hall, kitchen, sanctuary, balcony, basement or any unused nook. If there is not an inch of space in the church building, ask a church member who lives nearby to volunteer a living room or den for the class until permanent headquarters can be located.

Wherever the class meets, someone should be in charge of seeing that the meeting space is as attractive, practical, comfortable and inviting as possible. Be sure that chairs are arranged in a circle so that eye contact with all class members is possible.

207

Pathfinder:

This word is used instead of *teacher* for a couple of reasons. First, it indicates leadership, one of the most important characteristics of a good teacher, and second, it begins with the letter P and beats the heck out of pedagogue.

The committee should appoint a temporary teacher. After the class has become established, they may choose to ask that person to teach on a more permanent basis, but it is important for the group to feel they have a voice in who teaches them.

If ever there was a need for a super-deluxe, number one, first class, bang-up, Grade A, topnotch teacher, it is in a newly formed class. The teacher should be committed to the serious responsibility of doing everything possible to get the new class off and running.

Program of Study:

That's another way to say curriculum, lesson materials, or Sunday school literature. Here again, if possible, it's advisable for the group to have a voice in what it will be studying. Granted, some groups don't know enough to select appropriate lesson materials, but if it's practical, members of the group should help decide the study topic and books to be used.

Every effort should be made to determine the needs of the group and offer a study that will be likely to meet those needs. If class members don't feel that the subjects discussed are worthwhile and meaningful, they won't come back, and the new class will bite the dust before it ever gets off the ground.

Publicity:

Once decisions have been made concerning the classes' meeting place, time, teacher and study topic, there should be a publicity blitz. Make sure the word gets out that everyone is invited and will be welcomed warmly. (Then make sure they do feel welcome when they get there!)

Advertise the class in the church bulletin and newsletter. Send postcards to everyone on the prospect list. Members of the committee should call all prospects. Best of all, talk to prospective members face to face to issue the invitation. Use the church bulletin board to tell about the new class, and place posters throughout the church proclaiming the news.

The place where the class meets should be clearly marked.

A colorful poster that says "Come On In — This Is The So-And-So Class" might be placed in a highly visible spot outside the classroom. If the sign is on the door and the door is opened into the room, it might not be seen, and prospects could just walk right on by.

Party:

Sometime within the week before the first class meeting, have a party for all prospective members. A hamburger supper or something similar will provide the informal atmosphere that encourages a feeling of acceptance and belonging among the group.

Invitations to the party should be carefully, personally and courteously extended. Don't assume that anyone knows he's invited. If at all possible, get a definite commitment from people as to whether or not they'll attend the party, but don't let the necessity for an R.S.V.P. keep anyone away. It's better to have a few hamburgers left over than to make people feel they can't come at the last minute if their schedule permits.

Be sure that everyone wears a legible name tag. Save the name tags and see to it that people wear them for the first few Sundays or until the class members know everyone by name. (By all means keep the class on a first name basis!)

Activities for the party should be planned with the group in mind. If most of them don't know each other, have some get-acquainted ice breakers. If everyone present is already acquainted, they might enjoy chatting informally with no structured or planned entertainment.

Participation And Personal Care:

If the new class is going to fly, there must be participation by as many members as possible. Each person must feel that he is an important part of the group. The teacher can encourage participation by the choice of teaching methods and by creating a relaxed and friendly atmosphere.

Participation is increased when class officers are elected and committees named (through volunteering, not conscription). These officers and committees should take care of class business such as service projects and cards or calls to absentees, newcomers, the sick and bereaved.

It will be a while before a brand new class has much business to attend to, but the sooner people feel needed and valued by the group, the sooner they will develop loyalty to the group.

Persistence And Patience:

Sometimes groups are formed quickly, catch on like wildfire and grow by leaps and bounds. Usually it takes time. A patient, persistent teacher who is willing to put in hours of preparation time for the benefit of the four or five who show up will one day be rewarded by the presence of a roomful of eager learners.

Persistence and patience on the part of the core group

210

within the class is also necessary. They must persist in publicizing the group and inviting people to be a part of it. It is important for this persistence and patience to be joyful and optimistic. The attitude must be, "We may be small this week, but you just watch us grow!"

Protect Teaching Time:

Class business is important. Fellowship is important. Coffee is important (well, some people think it's important). But the reason for the class must be kept uppermost in everyone's mind. Don't let a discussion of the group's service project or news about who's had surgery and babies monopolize the hour. Protect teaching time by keeping announcements brief and delegating work to committees.

Quantity:

The best class in the world won't be meaningful to those who aren't there. Most people who are missing don't know they are missing, much less what they are missing. Someone must tell them there is a place for them in Sunday school. Someone must see to it that the chairs have people in them.

Quality:

A new class can be formed by following the above P's and Q's, but it won't amount to much if the lessons and class activities aren't based on sound theological and educational principles. Quality curriculum materials and teaching methods, along with genuine concern for the needs of group members will not only get a new Sunday school class off the ground, they will make the class soar to happy rewarding heights.

ATTENDANCE CAMPAIGNS

Beware of the attendance campaign. It can begin with a bang and then fizzle to a pitiful whimper. Or it can give a church a push that results not only in increased attendance but in growth as a community of faith. A successful attendance campaign can mean not only high numbers, but also deeper commitment on the part of individuals.

Attendance campaigns have been held in disdain by many because the emphasis has sometimes seemed to be in the wrong place. Critics have been quick to proclaim, "The church should not be in the numbers racket."

Those on the other side of the question answer, "Enrollment statistics represent people, and there's nothing wrong with using a gimmick to get them into a situation that could have a lasting effect on their spiritual lives."

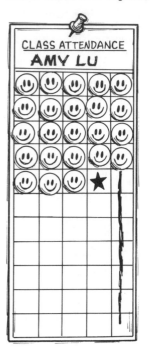

Supporters of Sunday school attendance campaigns will also point out that studies have shown that eight out of ten people who unite with the church enter through the doors of the Sunday school.

There are two kinds of attendance campaigns. One says, "Let's get 'em here." The other says, "Let's get 'em here and give them something when they get here that will have an ongoing and beneficial affect on their lives."

Assuming the latter approach is the one your church chooses, here are twelve tips to help you have a more successful attendance campaign.

1. Choose a leadership committee composed of enthusiastic, forward thinking individuals who are committed to the Sunday school and who will work tirelessly to make the campaign a success. Some people are natural leaders, and some are not. Be sure you get the ones who are.

2. Establish a specific propect list, but don't be limited by it. Brainstorm within classes for names of neighbors, relatives, business associates, etc. who are not in Sunday school. Check the church roll and pew registration cards for names. See if your local Welcome Wagon or Chamber of Commerce will share names of newcomers to the community.

3. Encourage friendly competition. Whether it should be inter-class or intra-class competition will depend on the number, size, ages and types of classes in your Sunday school. It may be necessary to compete on the basis of percentage increases rather than actual body count.

4. Duplicate and distribute written copies of the contest rules. This serves as a helpful reminder and can prevent mis-

understandings and hurt feelings. (Yes, believe it or not, that has been known to happen within the walls of the church!)

5. Set an ambitious but realistic goal and announce it.

6. Advertise and publicize through every available means. Letters, postcards, phone calls, church bulletin, newsletter, bulletin boards, posters, flyers, whatever you can do. However, the most effective method is eyeball to eyeball, person to person contact. "I want *You* to go with me" is far superior to "Everyone is invited."

7. Provide transportation if needed. If there is no church van or bus, enlist people who have station wagons and large cars to pick up visitors who need a ride. A special transportation committee should coordinate this. Everybody's business is nobody's business.

8. Have a kick-off program to begin the campaign on a definite date. Ask those who are enthusiastic about the Sunday school to make pep talks or testimonial comments concerning the importance of getting people to Sunday school. Explain the rules and encourage participation in a positive manner.

9. Give recognition and rewards to individuals and classes. Individuals could be awarded certificates, pins or other prizes. Classes could be given banners, certificates or even a "spirit stick." Recognition should be given on a weekly basis as part of the progress report.

10. Make it fun. Friendly rivalry should be invigorating and inspiring. If there is a positive, loving atmosphere, there can be no losers. Although one team or class will win the prize, banner or party, all will win when there is increased participation in the life of the church.

11. Provide quality Christian education in every Sunday school class. There's little point in getting people to come if there is not a meaningful experience, a learning opportunity, or warm Christian fellowship waiting for them when they get there. The attendance campaign is the time to encourage all teachers to do their very best and to make sure that classrooms and teaching equipment are in apple pie order.

12. Have a definite cut off date when the campaign is over. At that time, have a service of celebration and dedication to emphasize the fact that you are not at the end, but at the beginning of a period of renewed interest and participation in Sunday school. Be sure everyone is thanked graciously for all

work on the campaign. Recognize perfect attendance records, percentage increases, etc. Be sure that teachers and leaders in every class follow up and see that all new members are encouraged to become regular attenders.

HOW TO MAKE AN ATTENDANCE THERMOMETER

During a Sunday school attendance campaign, it's helpful to have a visible reminder of the progress being made. An "attendance thermometer" works well.

Each Sunday, the attendance is indicated by the rising red mark on the gauge. The thermometer can be made of cardboard, plywood, particle board or whatever material is available. The less ambitious may choose posterboard, but in most cases, something larger and more substantial is preferable.

Place the thermometer in a spot where it can't be missed. The hall where the heaviest traffic occurs is a good location. In some churches, the front of the sanctuary would be the logical choice. If you're brave and optimistic, make the thermometer weather-proof and put it on the church's front lawn.

Use figures that apply to your situation, but for now, let's pretend that your Sunday school has an average attendance of 125, and your goal for Sunday school attendance is 200.

"Calibrate" the thermometer with marks from 100 to 200 (see drawing). Paint the bulb and the area up to 100 red. Because it's too messy to get out a bucket of red paint each Sunday, and it takes too much time to fill in the thermometer with a red felt tip marker, use a strip of red fabric to indicate attendance growth. In order to do this, you'll need a slit cut in the thermometer through which the red fabric can be pulled up to the appropriate mark to indicate the day's attendance. The fabric can be thumbtacked at the correct point each Sunday.

Another advantage of using red fabric rather than paint is that if (heaven forbid!) attendance drops one Sunday, that can be easily exhibited.

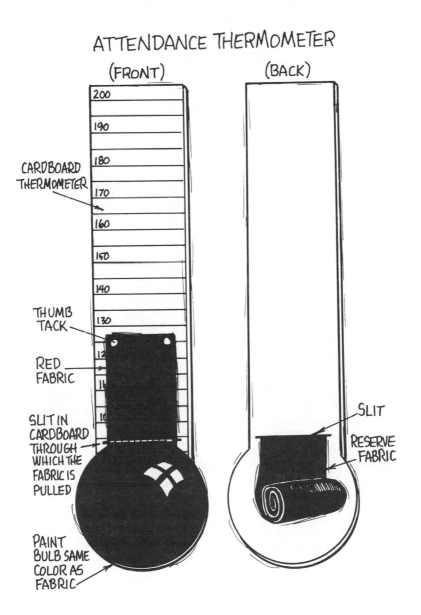

ATTENDANCE THERMOMETER

(FRONT)   (BACK)

CARDBOARD THERMOMETER

THUMB TACK

RED FABRIC

SLIT IN CARDBOARD THROUGH WHICH THE FABRIC IS PULLED

PAINT BULB SAME COLOR AS FABRIC

SLIT

RESERVE FABRIC

BIBLIOGRAPHY

Adair, Sharilyn. *Who is the Middle Elementary Child?* Workers With Children Series, Nashville: Board of Discipleship of the United Methodist Church, 1974.

Bible and You, The. South Deerfield, MA: Channing L. Bete Co., Inc.

Bogardus, Donna. *Children and the Bible.* Workers With Children Series, Nashville: Board of Discipleship of the United Methodist Church, 1974.

Bogardus, Donna. *I've Agreed to Teach Children.* Workers With Children Series, Nashville: Board of Discipleship of the United Methodist Church, 1973.

Bogardus, Donna and Frances Holliday. *Understanding Older Elementary Boys and Girls.* Workers With Children Series, Nashville: Board of Discipleship of the United Methodist Church, 1971.

Bower, Beth A. *The Joy of Teaching.* Nashville: Discipleship Resources, 1983.

Brooks, Frances M. *You Can Teach Anywhere if Necessary.* Department of Youth Publications of the United Methodist Church, Nashville: Graded Press.

Brown, Marion E. and Marjorie G. Prentice. *Christian Education in the Year 2000.* Valley Forge: Judson Press, 1984.

Calhoun, Mary. *Children Grow and Learn.* Workers With Children Series, Nashville: Board of Discipleship of the United Methodist Church, 1974.

Calhoun, Mary. *Our First/Second/Third Graders.* Workers With Children Series, Nashville: Board of Discipleship of the United Methodist Church, 1971.

Design for United Methodist Curriculum. General Board of Education of the United Methodist Church, Nashville: Graded Press, 1969.

Furnish, Dorothy Jean. *Exploring the Bible With Children.* Nashville: Abingdon, 1975.

Gable, Lee J. *Encyclopedia for Church Group Leaders.* New York: Association Press, 1959.

Glass, Dorlis and Martha Jones. *Where Are the Children?* Board of Discipleship of the United Methodist Church. Nashville.

Good Ways to Lead Adults. The Board of Christian Education of the Presbyterian Church, U.S.A. Richmond: John Knox Press, 1958.

Grimes, Howard. *Teaching Through Relationships.* Workers

With Children Series, Nashville: Board of Discipleship of the United Methodist Church.

Hampton, Peter J. *Children and Discipline.* Workers With Children Series, Nashville: Board of Discipleship of the United Methodist Church, 1974.

Hartman, Warren. *The Best Sunday School Teacher.* People to People Tabloid, Vol. I, Number 2, page 7, Nashville: Board of Discipleship of the United Methodist Church, Graded Press, Fall, 1985.

Hartman, Warren. *What Brings People Back?* People to People Tabloid, Vol. I, Number 1, page 1, Nashville: Board of Discipleship of the United Methodist Church, Graded Press, Summer, 1985.

Knoff, Gerald E. *The World Sunday School Movement.* New York: Seabury, 1979.

Little, Sara. *Learning Together in Christian Fellowship.* Richmond: John Knox Press, 1973.

Lynn, Robert W. and Elliot Wright. *The Big Little School —Two Hundred Years of the Sunday School.* Birmingham, AL: Religious Education Press, 1971.

Mass, Robin. *Church Bible Study Handbook.* Nashville: Abingdon, 1982.

McKean, Myra B. *What is a Kindergartner?* Workers With Children Series, Nashville: Board of Discipleship of the United Methodist Church, 1974.

Merjanian, Pepronia. *The Joy of Teaching.* Philadelphia: United Church Press, 1968.

Rice, Edwin W. *Sunday School Movement 1780-1917 and the American Sunday School Union 1817-1917.* Philadelphia: The American Sunday School Union, 1917.

Ryan, Roy H. *Educational Ministry With Adults.* Nashville: Board of Discipleship of the United Methodist Church. 1972.

Summers, Georgianna. *Teaching As Jesus Taught.* Nashville: Discipleship Resources, 1983.

Tillich, Paul. *Theology of Culture.* New York: Oxford University Press, 1959.

World Book Encyclopedia. Sunday School, Vol. 18, page 790, Chicago: Field Enterprises Educational Corp., 1977.

Zimmerman, Vera V. *Workers With Younger Children.* Nashville: Board of Education of the United Methodist Church, 1971.

ABOUT THE AUTHOR

The United Methodist Church recently honored Joanne Owens with the *Excellence in Education Award* as an outstanding Christian Educator in her district. That was a high point in her Sunday school teaching career, which began when she was in the kindergarden department, and she decided to teach the toddlers a thing or two.

Joanne received her Bachelor of Arts degree in Bible and Christian Education from Rhodes College (formerly Southwestern at Memphis), where she was considered somewhat strange because she taught Sunday school while all normal college kids slept in on Sunday mornings.

As Director of Christian Education at the First Presbyterian Church in Dalton, Georgia and the Whitehaven Presbyterian Church in Memphis, she taught Sunday school teachers how to teach, and she learned that the church's creme de la creme was found in the Sunday school.

When she became a Methodist by marriage, Joanne jumped right into the thick of things. Through the years she has served as a Sunday school teacher in every department, youth counselor, choir member, and chairman of a number of committees, including the Commission on Education and the Commission on Worship. She has held many offices in United Methodist Women, including president and district secretary.

Joanne now teaches an adult Sunday school class in Calhoun, Georgia, where she lives with her husband and three children on a dairy farm. When she is not studying her Sunday school lesson, she writes for a number of farm and religious publications.

When asked to comment on her busy schedule as a free lance writer and church leader, Joanne said, "The interests that I pursue provide challenge, creative outlets, inspiration, and continuing education for me, and besides, they all beat the heck out of milking cows."

Teachers Notes

Teachers Notes

*Following is a description of three
other Meriwether Publishing books that
will help you in planning Sunday school
activities.*

*For a complete free catalog of all
our books and plays write to:*
**Meriwether Publishing Ltd., Box 7710,
Colorado Springs, CO 80933**

COSTUMING THE CHRISTMAS & EASTER PLAY

by ALICE M. STAEHELI

Packed with photos and detailed illustrations, this exceptionally helpful book gives practical ideas and information on how you can costume almost any type of religious play on a limited budget. Costume designs are based on the authentic clothing styles of the period, but they're simplified to give you more time for important things like rehearsals. You'll also find drawings, photos, detailed dimensions and many suggestions about props, storage and handling of costumes. With this book, you'll find your dramatic productions take on a more professional look. This paperback book is available at bookstores or from Meriwether Publishing Ltd., P.O. Box 7710, Colorado Springs, Colorado 80933.

CELEBRATING SPECIAL DAYS IN THE CHURCH SCHOOL YEAR

by JUDY GATTIS SMITH

Why not involve these future church leaders further with liturgies and activities tailored for them? *Celebrating Special Days in the Church School Year* is packed with liturgies and ideas for commemorating holidays and church themes. Author Judy Gattis Smith has a rare feel for what children enjoy, so the activities she's included in this book are guaranteed to excite children and get them thinking. The programs and activities cover such themes as:

- the beginning of school
- teacher appreciation
- the celebration of children as church members
- National Bible Week
- Advent
- Christmas
- a sense of mission
- Human Relations Day
- confirmation
- Mother's Day
- Pentecost
- welcoming new members to church school

The liturgies are ready to go, but you can adapt them as needed. You'll like the planning ideas, too. This reference desk book is available at bookstores or from Meriwether Publishing Ltd., P.O. Box 7710, Colorado Springs, Colorado 80933.

THE YOUTH IN ACTION BOOK

by SHIRLEY POLLOCK

Your youth group's alive and growing, and your teens are working hard, but they are running out of new ideas for fellowship and service activities. *The Youth in Action Book* is bursting with energy, ready to open doors to a wonderful world of positive action. The activities it explores are sure to expand your teens' sense of self-confidence and service to others. It opens the way to involvement with people of all ages. You'll get specifics about being creative, stretching know-how and being an active part of the community. Ideas for service activities include:

- being a junior firefighter
- working with the mentally handicapped
- being kind to parents
- cleaning up parks and streams
- helping with the world hunger problem
- teaching/tutoring others

There's plenty more, but what's best about this book is the way it will inspire your teens to do more. Youth leaders and youth alike will get years of use out of this paperback book, available at bookstores or from Meriwether Publishing Ltd., P.O. Box 7710, Colorado Springs, Colorado 80933.

ORDER FORM

MERIWETHER PUBLISHING LTD.
P.O. BOX 7710
COLORADO SPRINGS, CO 80933
TELEPHONE: (719)594-4422

Please send me the following books:

_____**The Official Sunday School Teachers**   **$7.95**
Handbook #CC-B152
by Joanne Owens
An indispensable aid and barrel of laughs for anyone
involved in Sunday school activities

_____**The Clown Ministry Handbook**   **$7.95**
by Janet Litherland #CC-B163
The first and most complete text on the art of clown ministry

_____**Fund Raising for Youth**   **$7.95**
by Dorothy M. Ross #CC-B184
Hundreds of wonderful ways of raising funds for youth

_____**Something for the Kids #CC-B192**   **$6.95**
by Ted Lazicki
Fifty-two "front-row" sermons for children

_____**Youth Ministry from Start to Finish #CC-B193** **$7.95**
by Janet Litherland
A step-by-step approach to successful youth ministry

_____**What Works and What Doesn't in Youth**   **$7.95**
Ministry #CC-B103
by Nido Qubein
A motivational and inspirational book for youth ministry leaders

I understand that I may return any book
for a full refund if not satisfied.

NAME: _____

ORGANIZATION NAME: _____

ADDRESS: _____

CITY: _____ STATE: _____ ZIP: _____

PHONE: _____

☐ **Check Enclosed**
☐ **Visa or Master Card #**_____

Signature: _____
          (required for Visa/Mastercard orders)

COLORADO RESIDENTS: Please add 3% sales tax.
SHIPPING: Include $1.50 for the first book and 50¢ for each additional
          book ordered.

☐ *Please send me a copy of your complete catalog of books or plays.*